TODAY I AM LOVABLE

365 POSITIVE ACTIVITIES FOR KIDS

DIANE LOOMANS

H J KRAMER
STARSEED PRESS
TIBURON, CALIFORNIA

H J Kramer Inc.
P.O. Box 1082
Tiburon, CA 94920

Art Director: Linda Kramer
Editor: Nancy Grimley Carleton
Editorial Assistant: Claudette Charbonneau
Composition and Design: Morgan Brooke
Cover Design: Jim Marin/Marin Graphic Services
Cover Art: Kim Howard
Book Production: Schuettge & Carleton
10 9 8 7 6 5 4 3 2 1

Library of Congress Cataloging-in-Publication Data
Loomans, Diane. 1955-
        Today I am lovable : 365 positive activities for kids / by Diane
        Loomans.
        p.   cm.
        Summary : Presents a year's worth of positive thoughts and esteem
-building activities to promote healthy values in preteens.
        ISBN 0-915811-68-5 (trade paper)
        1. Self-esteem in children --Juvenile literature. 2. Optimism-
-Juvenile literature. [1. Self esteem. 2. Optimism.] I. Title.
BF723.S3L663   1996
158'. 1' 0834--dc20   95-4951
                                                                CIP
                                                                AC

HAPPY NEW YEAR!

IN RUSSIA, NEW YEAR'S DAY IS THE BIGGEST DAY OF THE YEAR, AND CHILDREN EXCHANGE GIFTS. WRITE DOWN THREE GOALS THAT YOU CAN REACH AS A GIFT TO YOURSELF THIS YEAR:

JANUARY 1

1.

2.

3.

THOUGHT FOR THE DAY: EACH NEW DAY IS A GIFT THAT I GIVE TO MYSELF.

JANUARY 2

HERE IS A GREAT IDEA TO MEMORIZE THAT WILL HELP YOU GIVE SELF-ESTEEM TO OTHERS:

TODAY **I** WILL REACH OUT **IN** A SPECIAL WAY. TODAY **I** WILL GIVE **T**EN COMPLIMENTS AWAY!

THOUGHT FOR THE DAY: **I** WILL MAKE THE MOST OF MY DAY TODAY.

2

SIGN YOUR NAME WITH YOUR NON-DOMINANT HAND (THE HAND YOU DON'T USUALLY USE FOR WRITING) AT LEAST THREE TIMES TODAY.

DOES IT FEEL UNCOMFORTABLE? **N**EW HABITS OFTEN FEEL THAT WAY IN THE BEGINNING. **S**TAY WITH THIS EXERCISE—OR BETTER YET, A NEW HABIT—FOR THREE WEEKS, AND IT WILL BEGIN TO FEEL NATURAL TO YOU!

JANUARY 3

THOUGHT FOR THE DAY: **W**ITH PRACTICE, WHAT ONCE SEEMED IMPOSSIBLE BECOMES POSSIBLE.

UNSCRAMBLE THE FOLLOWING SENTENCE:

JANUARY 4

ME LIKE QUITE ONE NO IS THERE WORLD THE ALL IN

THOUGHT FOR THE DAY:

I WILL NOTICE EVERYTHING THAT IS UNIQUE ABOUT ME TODAY.

ANSWER: THERE IS NO ONE QUITE LIKE ME IN ALL THE WORLD.

4

FAMOUS AUTHOR CHARLES DICKENS SAID,
"THE SUM OF THE WHOLE IS THIS: WALK
AND BE HAPPY, WALK AND BE HEALTHY!"

MAKE SURE YOU GET PLENTY OF
EXERCISE EACH DAY. WALK OR BIKE TO
SCHOOL, THE STORE, OR YOUR FRIENDS'
HOUSES WHENEVER YOU CAN. YOU'LL
FEEL GREAT AND HAVE MORE ENERGY!

JANUARY
5

HOW CAN YOU START TODAY?

THOUGHT
FOR THE DAY:

I WILL DANCE, PLAY, EXERCISE,
OR WALK TO FEEL GREAT TODAY!

SMILE
A LOT TODAY!

JANUARY
6

DID YOU KNOW THAT A SMILE IS ONE OF THE ONLY GESTURES THAT HAS THE SAME MEANING ALL OVER THE WORLD?
SMILE AT AS MANY PEOPLE AS YOU CAN TODAY, AND YOU WILL DISCOVER ONE OF THE GREATEST SECRETS IN THE UNIVERSE. **S**MILES ARE LIKE MAGNETS. **T**HEY ATTRACT POSITIVE PEOPLE, PLACES, AND THINGS TO YOU!

THOUGHT FOR THE DAY:

TODAY **I** WILL BE FRIENDLY TO EVERYONE **I** MEET.

6

KNOCK KNOCK.

WHO'S THERE?

PASTA.

PASTA WHO?

PASTA-TIVE MENTAL ATTITUDE,
THAT'S WHO!

THOUGHT FOR THE DAY:

TODAY I WILL NOTICE WHAT'S
GOING RIGHT WITH MY WORLD.

CREATE A "TREASURE MAP" FOR YOURSELF BY COLLECTING PICTURES AND WORDS FROM MAGAZINES THAT REPRESENT DREAMS AND WISHES THAT YOU HAVE.

PASTE THEM TOGETHER INTO A COLLAGE AND POST YOUR TREASURE MAP IN A PLACE WHERE YOU WILL SEE IT EVERY DAY.

THOUGHT FOR THE DAY: **I** MUST FIRST HAVE A DREAM IF **I** WISH TO HAVE A DREAM COME TRUE.

8

THIS ANCIENT EGYPTIAN SYMBOL IS CALLED AN **ANKH**. **I**T STANDS FOR LIFE. **Y**OU ARE RICHLY BLESSED WITH THE GIFT OF LIFE!

JANUARY 9

THOUGHT FOR THE DAY:

I WILL TAKE THE TIME TO NOTICE ALL OF THE LIVING THINGS AROUND ME (INCLUDING MYSELF!) AND GIVE THANKS TODAY.

GET A PACKAGE OF SEEDS AND GROW YOUR OWN VEGETABLE, FLOWER, OR OTHER PLANT IN A POT.

JANUARY 10

TEND TO IT. **E**NJOY IT. **L**OVE IT.
YOU, TOO, ARE LIKE A GROWING PLANT IN THE WORLD.
YOU NEED LOVING CARE TO THRIVE AND BE HAPPY!

THOUGHT FOR THE DAY: **T**ODAY **I** WILL ASK FOR SOME TENDER, LOVING CARE.

YOUR NEEDS AND WANTS ARE VERY IMPORTANT. **W**HAT IS SOMETHING THAT YOU WANT BUT HAVEN'T ASKED FOR? **F**ILL IN THE BLANKS WITH A FEW OF YOUR OWN NEEDS AND WANTS:

JANUARY **11**

WHAT **I** REALLY NEED RIGHT NOW IS

_____

I WANT TO FEEL MORE

_____

AND LESS

_____

WHAT **I** MOST WANT IS

_____

THOUGHT FOR THE DAY: **I** WILL LET SOMEONE KNOW ONE OF MY NEEDS OR WANTS TODAY.

HERE'S A GERMAN PROVERB THAT SPEAKS
ABOUT THE IMPORTANCE OF ORGANIZATION:

THOSE WHO BEGIN TOO MUCH ACCOMPLISH LITTLE.

JANUARY
12

HOW ARE YOU AT GETTING THINGS
DONE? IF YOU COULD USE SOME
IMPROVEMENT, ASK PEOPLE YOU
KNOW WHO ACCOMPLISH A LOT
HOW THEY DO IT.

THOUGHT FOR THE DAY: USEFUL TIPS CAN
SAVE A LOT OF TIME.

FIND THE CELEBRATION WORDS

Find and circle six words you might shout out loud when winning a game or achieving a goal.

H	E	R	X	E	Y
C	O	O	L	U	E
U	W	O	W	I	S
N	E	P	R	O	L
R	G	R	E	A	T
A	H	A	Z	T	Y

JANUARY

13

THOUGHT FOR THE DAY: EACH DAY **I** AM IMPROVING, GROWING, AND LEARNING!

ANSWER: HOORAY, YES, WOW, AHA, COOL, GREAT

THE PLANET IS BECOMING A **GLOBAL VILLAGE**, WITH PEOPLE OF ALL COUNTRIES BECOMING NEIGHBORS.

TACK UP A WORLD MAP IN YOUR ROOM. CHALLENGE YOURSELF TO LEARN TO IDENTIFY ONE NEW COUNTRY EACH DAY. MARK THE COUNTRIES THAT YOU WOULD LIKE TO VISIT IN YOUR LIFETIME.

BECOMING A "WORLD TRAVELER" WILL EXPAND YOUR HORIZONS!

THOUGHT FOR THE DAY: PEOPLE OF ALL COUNTRIES ARE MY GLOBAL NEIGHBORS.

I HAVE A DREAM . . .

—MARTIN LUTHER KING, JR.

MARTIN LUTHER KING, JR., HAD A DREAM OF EQUALITY FOR ALL PEOPLE, REGARDLESS OF THEIR RACE. THIS DREAM CARRIED HIM THROUGH ALL THE HARDSHIPS HE FACED STANDING UP TO BIGOTRY AND VIOLENCE.

THINK ABOUT WHAT YOUR DREAMS ARE TODAY. IF YOU DON'T HAVE A DREAM NOW, THINK ABOUT WHAT WOULD GIVE YOU HOPE FOR THE FUTURE AND WHAT YOU CAN DO TODAY TO START MAKING IT HAPPEN.

JANUARY 15

THOUGHT FOR THE DAY: TO DREAM A DREAM IS TO SPRINKLE SEEDS OF HOPE IN THE WORLD.

THE FIVE STAGES OF GROWING THROUGH A MISTAKE:

1. OUCH!
2. WHOA! OUCH!
3. HERE WE GO AGAIN ... OUCH!
4. HELP! HEY, I WANT ANOTHER WAY!
5. AHA! HOORAY! I FOUND A **BETTER WAY!!**

JANUARY 16

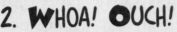

THOUGHT FOR THE DAY:

IF I'M NOT MAKING ANY MISTAKES, I'M PROBABLY NOT LEARNING VERY MUCH!

EXERCISE YOUR FUNNY BONE TODAY
BY ASKING SOMEONE TO ANSWER THIS
"QUACK QUESTION" OF THE DAY:

WHICH WOULD YOU RATHER
BE—A SMILE, A GIGGLE, OR
A BELLY LAUGH—AND WHY?

JANUARY 17

THOUGHT FOR THE DAY: I WILL TAKE THE TIME TO LAUGH AND HAVE SOME FUN TODAY.

17

DO YOU HAVE A PHOTOGRAPH OF YOURSELF THAT YOU REALLY LIKE? **I**F NOT, ASK SOMEONE TO TAKE SOME PICTURES OF YOU. **P**ICK YOUR FAVORITE AND PLACE IT IN A SPECIAL FRAME. **P**UT IT IN A SPOT WHERE YOU WILL SEE IT OFTEN.

JANUARY 18

WHEN YOU LOOK AT IT, SAY, "**I** WILL ALWAYS BE YOUR BEST FRIEND, NO MATTER WHAT!"

THOUGHT FOR THE DAY: **T**ODAY **I**'LL BE AS NICE TO MYSELF AS **I** WOULD BE TO MY BEST FRIEND.

LET YOUR FRIENDS AND LOVED ONES KNOW THEY ARE WELCOME IN YOUR HOME WITH A GREETING SIGN OR WORDS THAT SAY JUST THAT. HERE ARE A FEW WAYS TO WRITE OR SAY **WELCOME** FROM DIFFERENT PARTS OF THE GLOBE:

AFRIKAANS—**WELKOM** (VEL-KAHM)

GERMAN—**WILLKOMMEN** (VIL-KAHM-EN)

SPANISH—**BIENVENIDOS** (BEE-EM-BAY-NEE-DOS)

SWAHILI—**KARIBU** (KAH-REE-BOO)

JANUARY

19

THOUGHT FOR THE DAY:

WHEN **I** GREET PEOPLE WARMLY, **I** LET THEM KNOW THAT THEY ARE WELCOMED AND IMPORTANT.

19

DID YOU KNOW THAT YOU ARE OLDER
THAN YOU THOUGHT?
GET A CALCULATOR AND ASK SOMEONE TO
HELP YOU ANSWER THE FOLLOWING
STATEMENTS:

I AM _____ MONTHS OLD.

I AM _____ WEEKS OLD.

I AM _____ DAYS OLD.

I AM _____ HOURS OLD.

THOUGHT FOR THE DAY: **I** AM EVEN MORE AMAZING THAN **I** THOUGHT!

20

HAIKU (HI-KOO) ARE SHORT POEMS THAT ORIGINATED IN JAPAN IN THE 1600S. THEY FOLLOW A PARTICULAR PATTERN IN THREE LINES—FIVE SYLLABLES, SEVEN SYLLABLES, FIVE SYLLABLES. HERE'S AN EXAMPLE:

> WITH STRONG SELF-ESTEEM,
> I LEARN TO <u>FLY HIGH</u> AND <u>SOAR</u>—
> <u>AN EAGLE IN FLIGHT.</u>

NOW PICK THE ANIMAL YOU'RE MOST LIKE, AND MAKE YOUR OWN HAIKU BY REPLACING THE UNDERLINED WORDS.

JANUARY
21

THOUGHT FOR THE DAY:

THERE IS A WRITER IN EVERYONE JUST WAITING TO EXPRESS ITSELF.

INTERPRET THE FOLLOWING WORD PICTURE:

JANUARY 22

I SING

(HINT: IF YOU FEEL GREAT ABOUT SOMETHING
YOU DID, AND SOMEONE THANKED YOU FOR
IT BESIDES, THE THANK-YOU WOULD BE . . . .)

THOUGHT
FOR THE DAY:

TODAY I WILL SEE THE WORLD
THROUGH MY CREATIVE EYES.

DID YOU KNOW THAT IN PROPORTION TO THE REST OF ITS SIZE, THE GIRAFFE HAS A LARGER HEART THAN ANY OTHER MAMMAL? **B**ECAUSE THE GIRAFFE IS ALWAYS STICKING OUT ITS LONG NECK, A LARGE HEART IS NEEDED TO KEEP THE BLOOD FLOWING. **T**HERE IS A LESSON IN THIS FOR US HUMANS. **T**HE MORE WE REACH OUT TO OTHERS, THE "BIGGER" OUR HEARTS GET!

JANUARY 23

THOUGHT FOR THE DAY:

TODAY **I**'LL REACH OUT TO MORE PEOPLE — TO OFFER HELP AND TO GET HELP.

AN **ACRONYM** IS A WORD THAT IS FORMED FROM THE FIRST LETTERS OF TWO OR MORE OTHER WORDS. AN ACRONYM REPRESENTS AN ORGANIZATION OR IDEA: **M**OTHERS **A**GAINST **D**RUNK **D**RIVING (**MADD**).

CREATE AN ACRONYM OF YOUR OWN TODAY THAT EXPRESSES SOMETHING YOU BELIEVE IN STRONGLY. (TRY USING ONE OF YOUR NAMES!)

THOUGHT FOR THE DAY: TODAY **I** WILL BE A **C.O.O.L.** PERSON — CARING, OUTGOING, OUTSTANDING, AND LOVING!

24

DECODE THE FOLLOWING SYMBOLS AND PICTURES AND READ THIS STATEMENT ALOUD PROUDLY:

THOUGHT FOR THE DAY: WHETHER **I** CAN SEE IT OR NOT, **I** KNOW THAT THERE IS GREATNESS IN EVERYONE.

ANSWER: **I** AM A GREAT PERSON!

AN **IDIOM** IS AN EXPRESSION PECULIAR TO A LANGUAGE. THE MEANING MIGHT NOT MAKE SENSE LITERALLY, BUT IT GETS THE POINT ACROSS, OFTEN IN A COLORFUL WAY. HERE ARE THREE POSITIVE IDIOMS YOU CAN PRACTICE SAYING:

1. **I** HAVE **FLIPPED MY LID** OVER MY OWN BRILLIANCE!

2. **I** ASK FOR WHAT **I** WANT, RATHER THAN **BEAT AROUND THE BUSH!**

3. **I** IN MY MIND, NEW IDEAS ARE ALWAYS **ABOUT TO POP!**

THOUGHT FOR THE DAY:

TODAY **I** WILL SHOOT FOR THE STARS!

WRITE YOUR OWN PRAYER OR BLESSING
THAT DESCRIBES YOUR HOPE FOR THE WORLD
OR THE THANKS THAT YOU FEEL.
HERE IS AN EXAMPLE OF A VERY SIMPLE
PRAYER OF HOPE THAT SOME HINDUS
RECITE EACH MORNING:

JANUARY
27

MAY ALL BEINGS BE HAPPY.
MAY ALL BEINGS HAVE PEACE.

THOUGHT FOR THE DAY: EVERY BLESSING FOR THE
WORLD IS A DROPLET OF HOPE
IN AN OCEAN OF PEACE.

JANUARY 28

VINCE **L**OMBARDI WAS A FAMOUS FOOTBALL COACH WHO ONCE SAID, "**I**NCHES MAKE CHAMPIONS."

SOMETIMES IT'S THE LITTLE EXTRAS THAT WE DO FOR OURSELVES AND OTHERS THAT REALLY MAKE A DIFFERENCE.

THOUGHT FOR THE DAY: **T**ODAY **I** WILL BE AWARE OF THE LITTLE EXTRAS **I** CAN DO TO HELP MYSELF OR SOMEONE ELSE TO FEEL LIKE A CHAMPION.

FIND THE HAPPINESS WORDS BY UNSCRAMBLING EACH OF THE FOLLOWING:

RECHE

ERYRM

YOJ

STEZ

ELEG

YOLJL

JANUARY

29

THOUGHT FOR THE DAY: **WHEN I SPREAD JOY TO OTHERS, EVEN MORE OF IT RUBS OFF ON ME!**

29

WHEN YOU GO TO SLEEP TONIGHT, DECIDE TO REMEMBER AT LEAST ONE DREAM.

JANUARY 30

YOU WILL SURPRISE YOURSELF WITH HOW WELL YOUR MIND LISTENS TO YOUR REQUEST. **M**OST OF US DREAM FIVE TO SEVEN DREAMS PER NIGHT. **W**HY NOT LEARN TO REMEMBER ONE OR TWO, AND LEARN MORE ABOUT THE MOVIES THAT YOU ARE DIRECTING AND STARRING IN EACH NIGHT!

THOUGHT FOR THE DAY: **W**HEN **I** LEARN TO REMEMBER MY DREAMS, **I** UNDERSTAND MORE ABOUT MYSELF.

DID YOU KNOW THAT IN THE FUTURE, WE WILL SAVE MANY TREES BY USING FAR LESS PAPER? **E**LECTRONIC MAIL WILL BECOME MORE COMMON. **P**EOPLE CAN ALREADY READ MAGAZINES AND NEWSPAPERS, WRITE CHECKS, SEND AND RECEIVE MAIL, AND EVEN GO SHOPPING USING THEIR HOME COMPUTERS!

JANUARY
31

DO SOMETHING TO BECOME MORE "FRIENDLY" WITH COMPUTERS TODAY. **Y**OU'LL BE GLAD YOU DID!

THOUGHT FOR THE DAY: **T**ODAY **I** WILL LEARN SOMETHING NEW ABOUT COMPUTERS.

FEBRUARY 1

Have you ever considered beginning a list of your life ambitions? Seventy-year-old John Goddard wrote a list of 127 life goals when he was fifteen. Many of them were challenging, like climbing the world's major mountains, running a mile in five minutes, and reading an entire encyclopedia.

He has completed 107 of his goals, and he hasn't stopped yet!

THOUGHT FOR THE DAY:

Today I will practice thinking big by starting my own life goals list.

A **SIMILE** (**SIM**-UH-LEE) IS A FIGURE OF SPEECH THAT COMPARES TWO DIFFERENT THINGS USING **LIKE** OR **AS**; FOR EXAMPLE, "**S**HE WAS AS FAST AS A HORSE," OR "**H**E RUNS LIKE THE WIND." **F**ILL IN THE BLANKS BELOW USING SIMILES:

FEBRUARY

2

I AM AS HAPPY AS A _____.

I'M FEELING AS SMART AS A _____.

I AM AS CALM AS_____.

THOUGHT FOR THE DAY: **T**ODAY **I** WILL SOAR HIGHER THAN A KITE!

FEBRUARY

3

THE PLAINS INDIAN WARRIORS CARVED AN EAGLE ON THEIR SHIELDS FOR PROTECTION.

DRAW A POWER ANIMAL OF YOUR CHOICE INSIDE THE SHIELD, AND USE IT AS A SYMBOL OF PROTECTION AGAINST THOUGHTS THAT KEEP YOU IN FEAR.

THOUGHT FOR THE DAY: TODAY I WILL BE AWARE OF HOW MUCH POWER AND STRENGTH I HAVE INSIDE.

DID YOU KNOW THAT MOST PEOPLE THINK 40,000 TO 50,000 THOUGHTS A DAY? THAT'S A LOT OF THINKING, BUT HOW MANY OF THOSE THOUGHTS ARE HELPFUL?

FEBRUARY 4

CHECK IN DURING YOUR DAY TO SEE IF YOU ARE FOCUSING ON THE POSITIVE OR THE NEGATIVE. YOUR BRAIN IS LIKE A COMPUTER. HOW ARE YOU PROGRAMMING YOURS?

THOUGHT FOR THE DAY: I WILL LOOK FOR THE POSITIVE THINGS IN MY LIFE TODAY.

THIS IS THE ANCIENT **C**HINESE **YIN-YANG** SIGN, WHICH STANDS FOR THE OPPOSITES IN LIFE. **N**IGHT AND DAY, UP AND DOWN, LIGHT AND DARK, HAPPY AND SAD—THERE ARE MANY OPPOSITES THAT WE LIVE WITH EACH DAY.

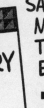

FEBRUARY

5

THE **C**HINESE BELIEVE THAT IT IS THE MARK OF A WISE PERSON TO APPRECIATE DIFFERENCES IN LIFE. **N**OTICE AND APPRECIATE THE OPPOSITE OF AT LEAST THREE THINGS IN YOUR LIFE TODAY.

THOUGHT FOR THE DAY: **T**HERE IS GOOD TO BE FOUND IN THE UPS AND THE DOWNS OF MY EVERYDAY LIFE.

GIVE THIS
HUG
CERTIFICATE
TO
SOMEONE
SPECIAL
TODAY.

FEBRUARY
6

This certifies that

_____

is lovable and
special, and is
entitled to free hugs
from

_____

(To be redeemed
anytime, day or night!)

THOUGHT
FOR THE DAY: TODAY I WILL GIVE AWAY
AT LEAST THREE HUGS!

FEBRUARY 7

WOULD YOU LIKE TO BECOME A BETTER FRIEND? ASK YOUR FAMILY AND FRIENDS FOR THREE WAYS THEY WANT TO BE LOVED, AND THEN SURPRISE THEM WITH THE GIFT OF ONE OF THEIR REQUESTS.

YOU WILL DISCOVER ONE OF THE GREATEST LAWS IN THE UNIVERSE:

GIVERS GAIN.

THOUGHT FOR THE DAY: TODAY I WILL DO SOMETHING SPECIAL THAT SOMEONE I LOVE WILL GREATLY APPRECIATE.

INTERPRET THE FOLLOWING WORD PICTURE:

FEBRUARY

8

(HINT: YOU MIGHT FEEL THIS WAY WHENEVER YOU REMEMBER HOW LOVABLE AND CAPABLE YOU ARE.)

THOUGHT FOR THE DAY: I WILL ACCOMPLISH SOMETHING THAT GIVES ME A BOOST TODAY!

ANSWER: SITTING ON TOP OF THE WORLD.

FEBRUARY 9

DO YOU HAVE YOUR OWN BEDROOM? MOST CHILDREN AROUND THE WORLD DON'T HAVE THE PRIVILEGE OF HAVING A SEPARATE ROOM JUST FOR SLEEPING.

IF YOU DO, OR EVEN IF YOU SHARE A ROOM WITH A BROTHER OR SISTER, DO YOURSELF A FAVOR ... TAKE CARE OF YOUR ROOM! CLEAN IT, DECORATE IT, STACK AND LABEL USEFUL STUFF IN BOXES WITH LIDS, AND RECYCLE THE THINGS THAT YOU NO LONGER WANT.

THOUGHT FOR THE DAY: TODAY I WILL DO SOMETHING TO IMPROVE THE APPEARANCE OF MY BEDROOM.

WRITE THE LETTERS OF YOUR FIRST
NAME IN CAPITAL LETTERS IN A VERTICAL
ROW. THEN AFTER EACH LETTER WRITE
A POSITIVE WORD THAT BEGINS WITH
THAT LETTER. USE A DICTIONARY IF
YOU NEED IDEAS. HERE'S AN EXAMPLE:

FEBRUARY
10

DYNAMIC
ADMIRABLE
NICE
INTELLIGENT
EXCITING
LOVABLE

THOUGHT
FOR THE DAY:

I CAN CHOOSE TO LOOK AT MY
GREAT QUALITIES TODAY, RATHER
THAN DWELLING ON THE PARTS OF
ME THAT ARE STILL UNDER REPAIR!

TODAY IS NATIONAL SCIENCE DAY, IN HONOR OF THOMAS EDISON'S BIRTHDAY.

FEBRUARY 11

IN HIS EIGHTY-FOUR YEARS, HE INVENTED 1,097 THINGS, INCLUDING THE PHONOGRAPH AND THE LIGHT BULB.

HE ONCE SAID, "GENIUS IS ONE PERCENT INSPIRATION AND NINETY-NINE PERCENT PERSPIRATION."

THOUGHT FOR THE DAY: I WILL WORK TO PUT MY CREATIVE THOUGHTS IN ACTION.

ABRAHAM **L**INCOLN WAS A MAN OF GREAT PERSISTENCE. **H**E FAILED IN BUSINESS, WENT BANKRUPT, LOST HIS FIANCEE TO DEATH, HAD A NERVOUS BREAKDOWN, AND LOST EIGHT ELECTIONS BEFORE BEING ELECTED **P**RESIDENT OF THE **U**NITED **S**TATES. **W**ITH EACH SETBACK, HE TOLD HIMSELF, "**I**T'S A SLIP AND NOT A FALL."

FEBRUARY
12

HIS LIFE TEACHES US THAT THERE IS NO FAILURE; THERE IS ONLY LEARNING.

THOUGHT FOR THE DAY:

TODAY **I** WILL LOOK AT A MISTAKE **I**'VE MADE, AND DISCOVER WHAT **I** CAN LEARN FROM IT.

43

FEBRUARY 13

TAKE A WALK WITH SOMEONE YOU TRUST. (GO WHERE THERE ARE LOTS OF NATURE SOUNDS IF YOU CAN.)

CLOSE YOUR EYES, OR WEAR A BLINDFOLD, AND LET YOUR PARTNER LEAD YOU BY THE HAND. BECOME AWARE OF THE SOUNDS AND SCENTS THAT FILL YOUR SENSES WHEN YOU ARE NOT FOCUSING ON YOUR SIGHT. YOUR ENVIRONMENT AND NATURE WILL COME ALIVE IN A WHOLE NEW WAY. BE SURE TO GIVE YOUR PARTNER A CHANCE TO HAVE A TURN TOO!

THOUGHT FOR THE DAY: TODAY I WILL APPRECIATE THE OUTDOORS WITH ALL OF MY SENSES.

HAPPY VALENTINE'S DAY!

SAY "I LOVE YOU" TO SOMEONE
IN A NEW LANGUAGE TODAY.
CHOOSE FROM THE FOLLOWING:

FRENCH—**Je t'aime** (ZHE-TEM)

GERMAN—**Ich liebe Dich** (IK LEE-BUH DIK)

DUTCH—**Ik houd van je** (IK HOOD VAN YE)

SWAHILI—**Ninaupenda** (NEE-NAH-U-PAYN-DAH)

FEBRUARY
14

THOUGHT FOR THE DAY:

TODAY **I** WILL TELL THE PEOPLE IN
MY LIFE HOW MUCH **I** LOVE THEM.

45

RECIPE FOR A FABULOUS FRIENDSHIP FEAST:

1 HEAPING HELPING OF HONESTY
2 CUPS OF CARING AND COMPASSION
1 BUNCH OF BELLY LAUGHTER
2 PINCHES OF PATIENCE AND POLITENESS

SEASON WITH SELF-ESTEEM AND BAKE UNTIL YOUR HEART RUNNETH OVER.

THOUGHT FOR THE DAY: I HAVE WHAT IT TAKES TO BE A FABULOUS FRIEND!

TAKE A GOOD LOOK AT YOUR HANDS.
DID YOU KNOW THAT MANY SCIENTISTS
THINK THAT YOUR FINGERS AND HANDS
(AND YOUR WHOLE BODY FOR THAT
MATTER) ARE COMPOSED OF ATOMS
THAT MAY ONCE HAVE BEEN PART OF
THE STARS?

FEBRUARY
16

YOU ARE AN AMAZING MIRACLE
FROM HEAD TO TOE.

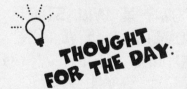

**THOUGHT
FOR THE DAY:**   **I** AM A LIVING PART
OF CREATION!

FEBRUARY 17

READ THE FOLLOWING CHINESE PROVERB, AND TALK TO SOMEONE ABOUT WHAT IT MEANS:

TO REMOVE A MOUNTAIN, BEGIN BY CARRYING AWAY SMALL STONES.

THOUGHT FOR THE DAY:

TODAY **I** WILL START SOMETHING **I**'VE BEEN PUTTING OFF BY TAKING A FEW SMALL STEPS.

ASK THE PEOPLE IN YOUR LIFE THIS "QUINTESSENTIAL QUESTION" FOR THE DAY:
WHICH WOULD YOU RATHER RECEIVE TODAY—A COMPLIMENT, A HUG, OR A SMILE—AND WHY?

FEBRUARY 18

AFTER YOU GET AN ANSWER, SURPRISE THEM BY GIVING THEM THEIR REQUEST!

THOUGHT FOR THE DAY:
I WILL REACH OUT TO SOMEONE WITH KINDNESS TODAY.

FEBRUARY 19

COMEDIAN VICTOR BORGE SAID THAT LAUGHTER IS THE SHORTEST DISTANCE BETWEEN TWO PEOPLE. KEEP THIS IN MIND TODAY AND FOLLOW THESE THREE TIPS:

1. GREET EVERYONE WITH A GRIN!
2. DON'T SWEAT THE SMALL STUFF!
3. REMEMBER, IT'S ALL SMALL STUFF!

THOUGHT FOR THE DAY: TODAY I WILL LAUGH OFTEN AND REMEMBER TO TAKE IT EASY!

THE ENGLISH WORD **GOOD-BYE** COMES FROM THE PHRASE "GOD BE WITH YOU." THE NEXT TIME YOU PART FROM A FRIEND, HERE ARE A FEW MORE WAYS TO SAY GOOD-BYE:

FEBRUARY **20**

SPANISH—**ADIOS** (AH-DEE-**OHS**)

FRENCH—**ADIEU** (AH-**DYUR**)

ITALIAN—**CIAO** (CHOW)

JAPANESE—**SAYONARA** (SAH-YO-**NAH**-RAH)

THOUGHT FOR THE DAY:

DOING SOMETHING DIFFERENT IS FUN FOR EVERYONE!

FEBRUARY
21

INTERPRET THIS
POSITIVE PHRASE,
WRITTEN IN
MORSE CODE:

```
··      ·-  --
··-   -· ··  --·-  ··-  ·
```

(LOOK ON PAGE 366 FOR THE
KEY TO DECODING MORSE CODE.)

**THOUGHT
FOR THE DAY**: **I** AM A ONE-OF-A-KIND!

ANSWER: I AM UNIQUE.

EIGHTY-FIVE-YEAR-OLD POET **N**ADINE **S**TAIR WROTE A POEM CALLED "**IF I HAD MY LIFE TO LIVE OVER AGAIN.**" **S**HE SAYS THAT SHE WOULD BE SILLIER, TAKE MORE TRIPS, RELAX MORE, CLIMB MORE MOUNTAINS, SWIM MORE RIVERS, PICK MORE DAISIES, AND DARE TO MAKE MORE MISTAKES. **D**ON'T WAIT UNTIL YOU'RE EIGHTY-FIVE TO REALIZE HOW PRECIOUS LIFE IS.

FEBRUARY
22

THOUGHT FOR THE DAY:

TODAY **I** WILL DARE TO TAKE A RISK AND HAVE FUN DOING IT!

53

FEBRUARY 23

SOMEONE ONCE SAID THAT EVEN A WATCH THAT DOESN'T WORK IS RIGHT TWICE A DAY! MANY OF US ARE AFRAID OF MAKING MISTAKES. SOME OF US FEEL ASHAMED WHEN WE DON'T HAVE THE ANSWER. BUT IT'S IMPORTANT TO REMEMBER THAT LIFE IS A BIG LEARNING LABORATORY.

MISTAKES ARE REALLY LESSONS!

THOUGHT FOR THE DAY: I WILL LEARN TO SEE MY MISTAKES AS ALLIES, NOT ENEMIES.

CROSS YOUR ARMS IN FRONT OF YOU WITH YOUR ELBOWS BENDING. LOOK DOWN TO SEE WHICH ARM IS ON TOP. NOW CROSS YOUR ARMS AGAIN, BUT THIS TIME MAKE SURE THE OTHER ARM IS ON TOP. IT PROBABLY FEELS A BIT DIFFERENT. DO THIS SEVERAL TIMES TODAY, UNTIL IT BEGINS TO FEEL FAMILIAR.

FEBRUARY
24

THOUGHT FOR THE DAY:

DOING SOMETHING NEW EACH DAY TAKES THE MENTAL BLUES AWAY!

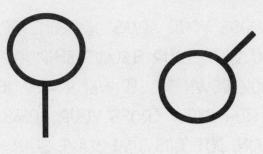

ADD A TOTAL OF THREE LINES TO COMPLETE THE SYMBOLS FOR **M**AN AND **W**OMAN.

IF YOU DON'T KNOW THE SYMBOLS, ASK SOMEONE TO HELP YOU!

THOUGHT FOR THE DAY: **T**ODAY **I** WILL CREATE MY OWN SYMBOL TO REPRESENT A SUCCESS **I**'D LIKE TO SEE HAPPEN.

KNOCK KNOCK.

WHO'S THERE?

ICON AND YUKON.

ICON AND YUKON WHO?

ICON DO IT, AND YUKON TOO!

FEBRUARY
26

THOUGHT FOR THE DAY: I WILL ENCOURAGE OTHERS I KNOW TO REACH THEIR GOALS TODAY!

FEBRUARY 27

HERE IS AN AWESOME QUESTION TO ASK SOMEONE TODAY: WHAT PERCENTAGE OF THE BODY IS REALLY EMPTY SPACE?

NOW, IF YOUR FRIENDS TELL YOU THEY FEEL "SPACEY," YOU CAN TELL THEM WHY!

THOUGHT FOR THE DAY: TODAY I WILL TAKE THE TIME TO NOTICE THE AMAZING WONDERS THAT SURROUND ME.

ANSWER: 99.9999 PERCENT!

AFTER EACH LETTER OF THE WORD
LOVE, WRITE A POSITIVE WORD
ABOUT WHAT LOVE MEANS TO YOU:

FEBRUARY
28

L _____

O _____

V _____

E _____

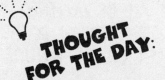
THOUGHT FOR THE DAY: **I** WILL SAY THE THREE MAGIC
WORDS TO SOMEONE **I** CARE
ABOUT TODAY: **I** LOVE YOU!

MARCH 1

WOULD YOU LIKE TO BE ABLE TO USE AN OLD **L**ATIN PHRASE? **I**T'S **"CARPE DIEM"** (CAR-PAY DEE-UM), WHICH MEANS, "SEIZE THE DAY," OR "LIVE NOW."

TEACH THIS PHRASE TO OTHER PEOPLE IN YOUR LIFE. **T**HEY WILL BE GLAD YOU DID!

THOUGHT FOR THE DAY: **I** WILL PUT ALL OF MY ENERGY INTO THE PRESENT TODAY, RATHER THAN THE PAST OR THE FUTURE.

DECODE THE FOLLOWING SENTENCE:

MARCH 2

 THOUGHT FOR THE DAY: MY THOUGHTS HELP TO MAKE MY WORLD WHAT IT IS.

ANSWER: I HELP CREATE MY WORLD.

MARCH 3

ASK SOMEONE THIS
"QUANTUM QUESTION"
FOR THE DAY:

WHAT WOULD YOU RATHER
DO—TRAVEL AT THE SPEED
OF LIGHT, RIDE ON A COMET,
OR TRAVEL THROUGH A
BLACK HOLE—AND WHY?

THOUGHT FOR THE DAY:

TODAY I WILL ASK AT LEAST
THREE UNUSUAL QUESTIONS
OF SOMEONE ELSE.

CAN YOU UNSCRAMBLE THIS FAMILIAR FOLK SAYING? (HINT: IT'S A TIP ABOUT SAVING TIME!)

MARCH

4

STITCH TIME A SAVES IN NINE

THOUGHT FOR THE DAY: I WILL NOTICE HOW I USE MY TIME TODAY.

MARCH
5

MOST OF US NEED TO BE NOTICED MORE OFTEN. WRITE A COUPLE OF FRIENDS A SHORT NOTE OF APPRECIATION TODAY.

TELL THEM THREE WAYS YOU APPRECIATE THEM.

YOUR EFFORT WILL BE TREASURED!

THOUGHT FOR THE DAY: THE GREAT GIFT OF APPRECIATION IS ALWAYS GREATLY APPRECIATED!

FIND AND CIRCLE THE MESSAGE HIDDEN
WITHIN THE LETTERS BELOW.
(HINT: IT'S SOMETHING THAT YOU
MIGHT SAY ABOUT YOURSELF WHEN
YOU ARE FEELING GREAT.)

MARCH
6

KOSTEBDPZCSHOORAYOCU

VUNNEYWRBKNHMMJIP

WOQDIDELPDITTS

THOUGHT
FOR THE DAY:

TODAY **I** WILL CELEBRATE
SOMETHING GREAT ABOUT
MYSELF THAT ONLY **I**
KNOW ABOUT!

ANSWER: HOORAY! I DID IT!

65

MARCH 7

WHEN YOU ARE TENSE, NERVOUS, OR SCARED, REMEMBER TO BREATHE SLOWLY. IT DOES WONDERS! HERE IS A SHORT POEM TO HELP YOU TO REMEMBER:

BREATHE IN A SLOW
AND RHYTHMIC WAY
TO FEEL RELAXED
ALL THROUGH THE DAY!

THOUGHT FOR THE DAY:

TODAY I WILL DO MY BEST TO STAY CALM AND RELAXED ALL DAY LONG!

SIGN YOUR NAME BACKWARDS TODAY.
IF YOUR NAME IS JOHN OR MARY,
IT MIGHT LOOK LIKE THIS:

MARCH
8

Mary

John

DOING THINGS DIFFERENTLY FROM TIME
TO TIME CAN KEEP YOU (AND EVERYONE
ELSE) AWAKE AND ALERT!

THOUGHT
FOR THE DAY:
TODAY I WILL DO SOMETHING
DIFFERENT TO KEEP ME ALIVE,
AWAKE, AND ALERT!

MARCH 9

YOU ARE TALENTED, AND IT'S OKAY TO FEEL GOOD ABOUT THE THINGS YOU DO WELL. NAME THREE OF YOUR TALENTS, AND THEN GIVE YOURSELF A PAT ON THE BACK!

1.

2.

3.

THOUGHT FOR THE DAY: TODAY I WILL LET MYSELF FEEL PROUD OF ONE OF MY TALENTS.

68

UNSCRAMBLE THE FOLLOWING WORDS
THAT TELL HOW YOU FEEL WHEN
YOUR SELF-ESTEEM IS HIGH:

MARCH 10

EVALI

TEDINCOFN

REFE

YPHAP

THOUGHT
FOR THE DAY:

WHEN **I** FEEL GOOD ABOUT MYSELF,
I HAVE MORE TO OFFER OTHERS!

ANSWER: ALIVE, CONFIDENT, FREE, HAPPY.

MARCH 11

ONCE THERE WAS A BOY WHO WAS PUT IN A ROOM FULL OF MANURE AND TOLD TO DIG HIS WAY OUT WITH A SHOVEL. INSTEAD OF COMPLAINING, HE SAID, "OH BOY— THERE'S GOTTA BE A PONY IN HERE SOMEWHERE!"

THOUGHT FOR THE DAY: I WILL LEARN TO LOOK FOR THE GOOD IN SOMETHING THAT SEEMS UNPLEASANT.

THIS **I**SLAMIC SYMBOL IS CALLED THE **WINGED HEART**. **I**T STANDS FOR FREEDOM.

MARCH
12

KEEP THIS IN MIND TODAY: **I** HAVE THE FREEDOM TO THINK MY OWN THOUGHTS AND HELP CREATE MY OWN FUTURE.

THOUGHT FOR THE DAY: **T**O HAVE THE FREEDOM TO CHOOSE IS THE GREATEST FREEDOM OF ALL!

MARCH 13

TODAY, NOTICE ALL OF THE PATTERNS IN THE THINGS AROUND YOU—TREE BARK, SNOWFLAKES, LEAVES, PINECONES, RIPPLES OF WATER, THE SIDE OF A BUILDING, OR THE IRIS (THE COLORED PART) OF AN EYE.

YOU'LL DISCOVER THAT LIFE IS AN ART-MUSEUM-IN-MOTION!

THOUGHT FOR THE DAY: **T**ODAY **I** WILL NOTICE ALL OF THE LITTLE THINGS THAT **I** USUALLY DON'T SEE.

TODAY IS ALBERT EINSTEIN'S BIRTHDAY!

MARCH
14

HE WAS A SCIENTIST, PHILOSOPHER, AND PEACEMAKER WHO WAS CONSIDERED ONE OF THE GREATEST GENIUSES OF OUR TIME. HE ONCE SAID, "I DON'T THINK I AM PARTICULARLY INTELLIGENT, JUST PASSIONATELY CURIOUS!"

THOUGHT FOR THE DAY: I WILL ASK QUESTIONS ABOUT WHAT I'M CURIOUS ABOUT.

MARCH 15

CREATE YOUR OWN UPBEAT DOODLE POWER PHRASE THAT GOES WITH THIS PICTURE:

(EXAMPLE: "I'M BURSTING WITH LIFE!")

THOUGHT FOR THE DAY: TODAY I WILL INSPIRE MYSELF BY DOING SOMETHING CREATIVE!

THE NEXT TIME OTHERS YOU KNOW WANT TO PROCRASTINATE (PUT THINGS OFF), GIVE THEM THIS—IT'S A ROUND TUIT. **T**HEN THEY WON'T HAVE ANY MORE EXCUSES TO SAY, "**I**'LL GET **AROUND TO IT** SOME OTHER TIME!"

MARCH
16

THOUGHT FOR THE DAY:

WHEN **I** DO IT TODAY, **I** CAN CELEBRATE IT TOMORROW!

MARCH 17

FILL IN THE LUCKY FOUR-LEAF CLOVER WITH FOUR OF YOUR FAVORITE GREEN THINGS!

HAPPY ST. PATRICK'S DAY!

THOUGHT FOR THE DAY: TODAY **I** WILL TAKE THE TIME TO THINK ABOUT SOME OF MY FAVORITE THINGS.

HERE IS A RIDDLE FROM THE BANTU
PEOPLE OF EAST AFRICA THAT WILL
EXERCISE YOUR IMAGINATION:

MARCH
18

WHAT IS THE WHITE HUT
THAT HAS NO DOOR?

MAKE UP YOUR OWN RIDDLE TO ASK
SOMEONE TODAY, AND KEEP YOUR MIND ALIVE!

THOUGHT
FOR THE DAY:

TODAY I WILL FLEX MY MENTAL
MUSCLES TO KEEP MY BRAIN FIT!

ANSWER: AN EGG.

MARCH 19

BE THANKFUL TODAY FOR THE FOUR VITAL ELEMENTS OF THE UNIVERSE. **O**NE GROUNDS US, ONE SETS US FREE, ONE WARMS US, AND ONE CLEANSES AND NOURISHES US. **W**E NEED THEM ALL TO SURVIVE. **C**AN YOU NAME THEM?

1.

2.

3.

4.

THOUGHT FOR THE DAY: **I** AM GRATEFUL FOR EVERYTHING THAT NURTURES ME.

DECODE THE FOLLOWING AFFIRMATION
THAT IS WRITTEN IN MORSE CODE.

(LOOK ON PAGE 366 FOR THE
KEY TO DECODING MORSE CODE.)

MARCH
20

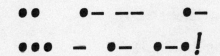

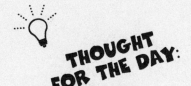

THOUGHT
FOR THE DAY:

TODAY **I** WILL SEE THE
GREATNESS IN MYSELF
AND OTHERS.

AT YOUR NEXT MEAL OR GATHERING, SURPRISE YOUR FAMILY OR FRIENDS BY SAYING "TO YOUR HEALTH" IN ANOTHER LANGUAGE! **H**ERE ARE A FEW EXAMPLES:

SPANISH—**SALUD** (SAH-**LOOD**)

DANISH—**PROOST** (PROAST)

SWEDISH—**SKAL** (SKOAL)

RUSSIAN—**NA ZADOROV `YE** (NAH ZDAH-**ROV** YAH)

THOUGHT FOR THE DAY: BEING HEALTHY IS A PRIVILEGE THAT **I** WILL NOT TAKE FOR GRANTED.

TODAY IS NATIONAL GOOF OFF DAY—
A DAY FOR GOOD-NATURED SILLINESS!

MARCH 22

WHEN YOU'RE OUT OF CLASS (AND WITHOUT BREAKING ANY SAFETY OR HOUSE RULES), LET YOUR INNER GOOF LOOSE TODAY—ACT LIKE A CLOWN, CROAK LIKE A FROG, SCREAM LIKE AN APE, OR TALK LIKE AN ENGLISH WAITER AT THE DINNER TABLE!

THOUGHT FOR THE DAY: TODAY I WILL LET MY INNER GOOF LOOSE, AND INVITE OTHERS TO DO THE SAME.

MARCH 23

All of us get scared sometimes, but did you know that 95 percent of what we fear never happens? Here's a way to think about most fears to help you through your day:

FALSE

EVIDENCE

APPEARING

REAL

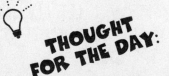

THOUGHT FOR THE DAY: Today I will face a fear with courage.

THIS IS THE INTERNATIONAL SIGN FOR LOVE.

MARCH
24

PRACTICE MAKING THIS SIGN WITH YOUR FAMILY AND FRIENDS WHEN GREETING THEM OR LEAVING.

THOUGHT FOR THE DAY:

I WILL SHOW SOMEONE **I** KNOW HOW MUCH **I** CARE TODAY.

MARCH 25

TAKE SOME TIME TO EXPLORE OUT IN NATURE OR AROUND YOUR NEIGHBORHOOD.

FIND A LARGE, SMOOTH ROCK. PAINT IT WITH ONE OF YOUR FAVORITE POSITIVE SYMBOLS OR WORDS, AND USE IT AS A PAPERWEIGHT, DOORSTOP, OR DECORATION, OR GIVE IT TO SOMEONE AS A GIFT.

THOUGHT FOR THE DAY:

TODAY I WILL TAKE THE ORDINARY AND MAKE IT EXTRAORDINARY!

THIS IS A "QUITE A QUESTION" TO ASK SOMEONE TODAY:

MARCH
26

WHICH WOULD YOU RATHER DO— FLOAT LIKE A CLOUD, FLOW LIKE A RIVER, OR DANCE LIKE A FLAME— AND WHY?

THOUGHT FOR THE DAY: **ASKING** QUESTIONS KEEPS MY MIND SHARP AND ALERT!

MARCH 27

OUR THOUGHTS ARE A LOT LIKE RADIO STATIONS. **C**HECK WHICH WAVELENGTH YOU LISTEN TO:

WHYN—FOR COMPLAINERS

WHOA—FOR THOSE WHO WORK TOO HARD

WONT—FOR NEGATIVE THINKERS

WHEE—FOR THOSE WHO ENJOY LIFE!

THOUGHT FOR THE DAY: **T**ODAY **I** WILL CHOOSE TO TUNE INTO THOUGHTS THAT UPLIFT ME.

IN SLOVAKIA AND THE CZECH REPUBLIC, TODAY IS TEACHERS DAY!

THINK OF YOUR FAVORITE TEACHER AND WRITE DOWN THREE THINGS YOU LIKE BEST ABOUT HIM OR HER:

MARCH 28

1.

2

3.

IF POSSIBLE, WRITE A THANK-YOU NOTE TO EXPRESS YOUR APPRECIATION!

THOUGHT FOR THE DAY:

I WILL WRITE A THANK-YOU NOTE TO EXPRESS MY APPRECIATION OF SOMEONE TODAY.

AN OXYMORON (AWK-SEE-MO-RON) IS A PHRASE WHOSE PARTS CONTRADICT EACH OTHER, FOR EXAMPLE: **PLAYFULLY SERIOUS, OUTRAGEOUSLY QUIET.**

MARCH 29

FILL IN TWO OXYMORONS OF YOUR OWN THAT DESCRIBE SOMETHING ABOUT YOU:

1.

2.

THOUGHT FOR THE DAY: TODAY **I** WILL HAVE AN "AWFULLY GOOD" DAY!

CREATE A BLOCK LETTER
TO SAY "I LOVE YOU"
TO SOMEONE.

MARCH
30

HERE IS AN EXAMPLE
OF HOW IT WORKS:

DEAR DAD — JUST WANTED — TO TELL YOU — YOU ARE THE — BEST!

THOUGHT FOR THE DAY: EVERYBODY NEEDS TO BE LOVED BY SOMEBODY TO FEEL LIKE ANYBODY!

MARCH 31

FACE A FRIEND AND
HOLD HANDS. SLOWLY
LEAN BACK UNTIL YOU ARE BOTH LEANING BACK,
HOLDING EACH OTHER UP. GOOD FRIENDS REACH
OUT TO ONE ANOTHER AND HELP KEEP EACH
OTHER FROM FALLING WHEN THEY CAN!

THOUGHT FOR THE DAY: TODAY I WILL OFFER MY HELP TO SOMEONE IN NEED.

ASK SOMEONE THIS
"INVENTION INTENTION" QUESTION TODAY:

IF YOU COULD INVENT **ANYTHING AT ALL** THAT WOULD MAKE THE WORLD A BETTER PLACE, WHAT WOULD IT BE, AND WHY?

APRIL 1

MAKE SURE THAT YOU ANSWER THE QUESTION YOURSELF ALSO!

THOUGHT FOR THE DAY:
I AM CAPABLE OF MORE THAN I REALIZE!

FIVE-YEAR-OLD **A**LICE WAS DRAWING IN HER KINDERGARTEN CLASS.

"**I**'M DRAWING **G**OD," SHE SAID TO HER TEACHER PROUDLY.

"**N**O ONE KNOWS WHAT **G**OD LOOKS LIKE," HER TEACHER SAID.

"**T**HEY DON'T? **W**ELL, THEY WILL WHEN **I**'M DONE!" SHE SAID.

DO YOU APPRECIATE YOUR OWN IDEAS ABOUT LIFE?

THOUGHT FOR THE DAY: **M**Y OWN **G**OOD IDEAS HELP TO MAKE THE WORLD A BETTER PLACE!

FILL IN THE MISSING LETTERS TO
DISCOVER SIX THINGS YOU CAN DO
TO CLIMB THE LADDER OF SUCCESS
WITH FRIENDS AND FAMILY:

APRIL
3

1. L _ _ T _ N   4. _ M _ L _

2. W R _ _ E   5. S _ A _ E

3. C _ _ E   6. G _ V _

THOUGHT
FOR THE DAY:

TODAY **I** WILL SPEND SPECIAL
TIME WITH THOSE **I** LOVE.

ANSWER: LISTEN, WRITE, CARE, SMILE, SHARE, GIVE.

YOUR FEELINGS MATTER—ALL OF THEM! WRITE DOWN A FEELING THAT DESCRIBES EACH FACE, AND THEN CHECK THE ONE THAT MOST SHOWS HOW YOU'RE FEELING NOW:

THOUGHT FOR THE DAY: TODAY I WILL NOTICE MY FEELINGS AND ASK FOR SOMETHING I NEED.

DECODE THE **E-Z** SECRET LANGUAGE.

IF YOU NEED HELP, SEE THE SECRET LANGUAGE DECODER ON PAGE 369.

APRIL
5

EZI EZAM EZA GEZIFT TEZO EZALL EZOF MEZY FREZIENDS.

THOUGHT FOR THE DAY: **M**Y FRIENDS ARE AMONG MY GREATEST TREASURES.

ANSWER: I AM A GIFT TO ALL OF MY FRIENDS.

95

APRIL

6

PEACE IS THE WORLD'S GREATEST DREAM! **F**OR EACH LETTER, FILL IN A WORD THAT DESCRIBES HOW YOU WILL FEEL IN A PEACEFUL WORLD:

P _____

E _____

A _____

C _____

E _____

THOUGHT FOR THE DAY:

TODAY **I** WILL TAKE FIVE MINUTES TO IMAGINE A PEACEFUL WORLD.

TODAY IS WORLD HEALTH DAY.

APRIL
7

ASK SOMEONE THIS "QUALITY QUESTION" TODAY:

WHAT IS THE MOST VALUABLE TREASURE YOU WILL EVER POSSESS THAT DOESN'T COST ANYTHING TO OWN, BUT NEEDS A LOT OF MAINTENANCE?

THOUGHT FOR THE DAY: TO HAVE HEALTH IS TO HAVE WEALTH!

ANSWER: YOUR HEALTH.

97

APRIL 8

YOU'LL BE SURPRISED BY THESE TWO ANSWERS:

HOW MANY MUSCLES DOES IT TAKE TO SMILE? _____

HOW MANY MUSCLES DOES IT TAKE TO FROWN? _____

FILL IN THE BLANKS WITH YOUR GUESSES!

THOUGHT FOR THE DAY: **A** SMILE IS SOMETHING THAT EVERYBODY SAYS IN THE SAME LANGUAGE.

ANSWER: 14 TO SMILE. 72 TO FROWN.

THE FUTURE BELONGS TO THOSE WHO BELIEVE IN THE BEAUTY OF THEIR DREAMS.

ELEANOR ROOSEVELT

APRIL 9

THOUGHT FOR THE DAY:

TODAY I WILL DESCRIBE ONE OF MY DREAMS TO A FRIEND, IMAGINING THAT IT HAS ALREADY COME TRUE.

APRIL
10

WHY DID THE BOLD
CHICKEN GO ONLY
HALFWAY ACROSS
THE ROAD?

**THOUGHT
FOR THE DAY**: **I** CAN TAKE A STAND
FOR WHAT **I** BELIEVE IN.

ANSWER: TO LAY IT ON THE LINE.

100

RUB YOUR HAND IN A CIRCLE ON YOUR STOMACH, PAT YOUR OTHER HAND ON THE TOP OF YOUR HEAD, AND SEE IF YOU CAN SAY, "**I'**M FULL OF GOOD IDEAS ALL OVER!" AT THE SAME TIME.

APRIL 11

THIS WILL IMPROVE YOUR COORDINATION AND YOUR ATTITUDE ALL AT ONCE!

THOUGHT FOR THE DAY: **S**OMETIMES THE ONLY WAY TO FIND OUT HOW TO DO SOMETHING IS TO TRY IT!

APRIL 12

UNSCRAMBLE THE FOLLOWING SENTENCE ABOUT YOURSELF:

EM MA I
TATH DALG
I MA

THOUGHT FOR THE DAY: THERE IS NO ONE I'D RATHER BE THAN ME!

ANSWER: I AM GLAD THAT I AM ME

102

THIS IS THE UNIVERSAL HAND
OF FRIENDSHIP SIGN THAT IS
USED IN MANY COUNTRIES AS
A SYMBOL OF HARMONY.

APRIL
13

DRAW IT ON
YOUR NEXT
PAPER OR LETTER
TO SOMEONE
SPECIAL.

**THOUGHT
FOR THE DAY**:

WHEN **I** SPEAK FROM THE HEART,
THE MESSAGE GOES A LONG WAY!

APRIL 14

MARK **T**WAIN ONCE SAID, "**I**F YOU TELL THE TRUTH, YOU DON'T HAVE TO REMEMBER ANYTHING ELSE." **A**LWAYS BE AS HONEST AS YOU CAN. **I**T'S A GREAT SKILL TO HAVE, AND IT WILL BUILD YOUR SELF-ESTEEM!

THOUGHT FOR THE DAY: WHEN **I**'M HONEST, **I**'M BEING ME—AND THAT'S GOOD ENOUGH.

APRIL IS KEEP AMERICA BEAUTIFUL MONTH!

APRIL 15

PICK UP LITTER; RECYCLE YOUR TRASH, PAPER, AND GLASS; AND PLANT FLOWERS OR TREES IN YOUR YARD OR NEIGHBORHOOD. THESE ARE JUST A FEW OF THE WAYS YOU CAN TAKE PRIDE IN YOUR ENVIRONMENT.

THOUGHT FOR THE DAY: **I** AM RESPONSIBLE FOR KEEPING MY ENVIRONMENT CLEAN AND BEAUTIFUL!

APRIL 16

DO YOU EVER USE **POWER TALK?** IT'S EASY! PICK A POSITIVE PHRASE AND SAY IT OVER AND OVER WHILE YOU WALK, RUN, PEDAL, JUMP ROPE, SKATE, OR DRIBBLE A BALL. HERE'S ONE YOU CAN USE, OR MAKE UP YOUR OWN!

I AM SMART, I AM STRONG. I FEEL CONFIDENT ALL DAY LONG!

THOUGHT FOR THE DAY: TODAY I WILL USE POWER TALK TO GET MYSELF FIRED UP!

IF YOU WANT TO FEEL REALLY INTELLIGENT, ASK SOMEONE THE FOLLOWING QUESTION:

HOW MANY LANGUAGES ARE THERE AROUND THE GLOBE?

APRIL 17

MOST PEOPLE WILL SAY, "I DON'T KNOW." ANSWER THEM WITH, "IF YOU DID KNOW, HOW MANY WOULD IT BE?"

THOUGHT FOR THE DAY:

THE WORLD IS FILLED WITH INTERESTING THINGS TO LEARN ABOUT!

ANSWER: 5,000.

APRIL 18

FILL IN THE FOLLOWING SENTENCE WITH YOUR OWN POSITIVE WORDS:

TODAY I WILL TELL MYSELF

_____ _____ _____ ,

I WILL NOTICE _____ _____ ,

AND I WILL REALLY

_____ _____ _____ !

THOUGHT FOR THE DAY: THINKING POSITIVELY IS A GREAT WAY TO START MY DAY!

WRITE FOUR OF YOUR HOPES FOR THE WORLD BELOW:

APRIL
19

 THOUGHT FOR THE DAY: **EACH DAY I WILL CARRY A TORCH OF HOPE FOR A BETTER WORLD.**

APRIL
20

UNSCRAMBLE THE FOLLOWING WORDS
THAT DESCRIBE HOW YOU MIGHT FEEL
WHEN YOU ARE IN A COURAGEOUS
MOOD:

EVARB

GONRST

DERIF PU

ERSU

THOUGHT FOR THE DAY: COURAGE IS FEAR THAT
HAS SAID ITS PRAYERS.

ANSWER: BRAVE, STRONG, FIRED UP, SURE.

CAN YOU GUESS
THIS WELL-KNOWN
FOLK SAYING ABOUT
STAYING HEALTHY?

APRIL
21

A. A. A. D. K. T. D. A.

THOUGHT FOR THE DAY: **I** WILL EAT HEALTHY FOOD TO STAY HEALTHY.

ANSWER: AN APPLE A DAY KEEPS THE DOCTOR AWAY.

APRIL 22

HERE IS A **S**IOUX **I**NDIAN WISH TO KEEP IN MIND TODAY TO HELP YOU BE MORE UNDERSTANDING OF OTHERS:

MAY **I** NOT JUDGE PEOPLE UNTIL **I** HAVE WALKED A MILE IN THEIR MOCCASINS.

THOUGHT FOR THE DAY: EVERYBODY HAS THE SAME BASIC NEED TO LOVE AND BE LOVED.

THIS HINDU SYMBOL IS A BLESSING CALLED **NAMASTE** (NUM-UH-STAY). IT MEANS "**I** SALUTE THE DIVINE IN YOU."

APRIL
23

MOST HINDUS PLACE THEIR PALMS TOGETHER AND NOD THEIR HEADS SLIGHTLY WHILE SAYING THIS AS A GREETING OR WHEN DEPARTING. TRY IT WITH SOMEONE YOU KNOW!

THOUGHT FOR THE DAY: TODAY **I** WILL SEE THE BEAUTY IN EVERYONE **I** MEET!

ASK A FRIEND THIS QUESTION TODAY:

IF YOU COULD SPEND THE REST OF YOUR LIFE IN THE PAST, PRESENT, OR FUTURE, WHERE WOULD YOU BE, AND WHY?

THOUGHT FOR THE DAY: **I** SHAPE MY PAST, PRESENT, AND FUTURE BY THE THOUGHTS **I** THINK.

EVERYONE NEEDS HEROES! THINK OF THREE PEOPLE YOU RESPECT AND WANT TO BE LIKE IN SOME WAY WHEN YOU GROW UP. WRITE THEIR NAMES BELOW. (YOU CAN CHOOSE FAMOUS PEOPLE OR PEOPLE YOU KNOW.)

APRIL
25

1.

2.

3.

THOUGHT FOR THE DAY: TODAY I WILL LOOK FOR THE HERO IN MYSELF AND OTHERS.

BE IN THE "FRIENDLY FRAME OF MIND" ALL DAY TODAY.

SMILE AT EVERYONE YOU CAN, AND SHARE KIND WORDS. **Y**OU'LL BE AMAZED BY HOW GREAT YOU'LL FEEL BY THE END OF THE DAY!

 **THOUGHT FOR THE DAY:** WHEN **I** GIVE TO OTHERS, **I** GAIN EVEN MORE MYSELF.

CREATE YOUR OWN POEM BELOW:

APRIL 27

____ ____ ____ YOU

____ ____ ____ ____TRUE

____ ____ ____ WAY

____ ____ ____ ____ DAY!

THOUGHT FOR THE DAY: ALL OF US HAVE A POET JUST WAITING TO EXPRESS ITSELF.

APRIL
28

WHAT MAMMAL IS THE MOST POSITIVE ANIMAL IN THE WHOLE WORLD?

THOUGHT FOR THE DAY: I AM AS HAPPY AS I MAKE UP MY MIND TO BE.

ANSWER: A HAPPY-POTAMUS.

HOW MANY DIFFERENT TREES CAN YOU IDENTIFY BY NAME? **G**O TO THE LIBRARY, TAKE OUT A BOOK ABOUT TREES, AND LEARN MORE ABOUT THESE MAGNIFICENT TREASURES ON OUR PLANET. **P**ICK A SPECIAL TREE IN YOUR YARD OR NEIGHBORHOOD TO NOTICE AND APPRECIATE, AND CONSIDER PLANTING A TREE!

APRIL
29

THOUGHT FOR THE DAY: **I** WILL ENJOY THE LIFE ALL AROUND ME.

APRIL 30

BREAKFAST IS A VERY IMPORTANT MEAL. **Y**OUR BODY NEEDS FUEL EACH MORNING TO START YOUR DAY IN A HEALTHY WAY. **H**ERE'S WHAT KIDS EAT FOR BREAKFAST IN OTHER PARTS OF THE WORLD:

SCOTLAND—OATS
CHINA—FRIED BREAD
JAPAN—RICE SOUP

THOUGHT FOR THE DAY: **I** WILL EAT WELL TO FEEL GOOD TODAY.

TODAY IS INTERNATIONAL LABOR DAY.

MAY 1

ALL OVER THE WORLD, PEOPLE WORK TO PROVIDE FOR THEIR FAMILIES. FIND A SPECIAL WAY TO THANK THOSE WHO PROVIDE YOU WITH FOOD, CLOTHES, AND SHELTER. MAKE A MEAL, WRITE A POEM OF THANKS, OR GIVE EXTRA HUGS, AND LET THEM KNOW HOW MUCH YOU APPRECIATE IT.

THOUGHT FOR THE DAY: TODAY I WILL DO MY WORK IN A SPIRIT OF JOY!

MAY 2

WE CAN THINK ABOUT OURSELVES AS HAVING FOUR DIMENSIONS OR PARTS.

CAN YOU GUESS WHAT EACH OF THE FOUR LETTERS STANDS FOR?

PAY ATTENTION TO HOW ALL YOUR PARTS SHOW THEMSELVES IN YOU.

THOUGHT FOR THE DAY: **T**ODAY **I** WILL CARE FOR ALL FOUR DIMENSIONS OF MYSELF — MY BODY, MIND, SPIRIT, AND FEELINGS.

ANSWER: BODY, MIND, FEELINGS, SPIRIT.

DECODE THE FOLLOWING WORD PICTURE TO DISCOVER SOMETHING THAT YOU ARE AND ALWAYS WILL BE.

MAY

3

x -

ordinary

THOUGHT FOR THE DAY:

I WILL BRING OUT MORE OF MY OWN INNER EXCELLENCE TODAY AND EVERY DAY.

ANSWER: EXTRAORDINARY

MAY 4

PABLO **P**ICASSO, THE GREAT **S**PANISH ARTIST, BROKE A LOT OF RULES WITH HIS ART WORK. **H**E EXPERIMENTED WITH A STYLE OF PAINTING CALLED **CUBISM**, IN WHICH HE STACKED EYES, REARRANGED BODY PARTS, AND DREW MORE THAN TWO EARS!

HE SAID, "**I** PAINT OBJECTS AS **I** THINK THEM, NOT AS **I** SEE THEM."

THOUGHT FOR THE DAY: **T**ODAY **I** WILL BE BOLD LIKE **P**ICASSO AND SHOW MY OWN STYLE!

HERE ARE SOME WAYS THAT YOU CAN USE SIMILES TO GIVE SOMEONE A COMPLIMENT TODAY:

MAY 5

1. YOU'RE AS COOL AS A CUCUMBER.

2. YOU'RE AS GENTLE AS A DEER.

3. YOU'RE AS CLEVER AS A _____.

4. YOU'RE AS SWEET AS_____.

THOUGHT FOR THE DAY: ALL LIVING THINGS NEED TO BE NOTICED AND APPRECIATED.

MAY 6

HERE'S ANOTHER "DO-SOME-THING-DIFFERENTLY-TODAY" EXERCISE TO HELP YOU SEE THE WORLD IN A NEW AND DIFFERENT WAY:

TRY WALKING BACKWARDS TODAY IN YOUR HOUSE AND SEE HOW IT FEELS, OR ESCORT SOMEONE ELSE TO GO FOR A WALK BACKWARDS WITH YOU.

THOUGHT FOR THE DAY: **C**HANGE IS GOOD FOR EVERYONE!

DECODE THE FOLLOWING
AFFIRMATION THAT IS
WRITTEN IN **M**ORSE CODE:

MAY

7

LOOK ON PAGE 366
FOR THE KEY.

••   •— ——

•—••   ———   ••• —   •—   —•••   •—••   •

THOUGHT
FOR THE DAY:

I AM LOVED BECAUSE OF
WHO **I** AM, RATHER THAN
WHAT **I** DO.

MAY 8

DID YOU KNOW THAT FAMOUS BASEBALL PLAYER **B**ABE **R**UTH HIT 714 HOME RUNS? **T**HAT SOUNDS IMPRESSIVE, BUT MANY PEOPLE DON'T REALIZE THAT HE ALSO STRUCK OUT 1,330 TIMES!

IT ISN'T FAILING THAT WILL HURT YOU; IT'S FAILING TO TRY AND TRY AGAIN. **B**ABE **R**UTH KEPT GOING, AND SO CAN YOU!

THOUGHT FOR THE DAY: **T**ODAY **I** WILL BELIEVE IN SOMETHING EVEN WHEN **I** CANNOT YET SEE IT!

FILL IN EACH LETTER OF THE WORD **FRIEND** WITH A WORD ABOUT WHAT ONE OF YOUR CLOSE FRIENDS MEANS TO YOU:

MAY 9

F_____

R_____

I_____

E_____

N_____

D_____

THOUGHT FOR THE DAY: FRIENDS ARE LIKE FLOWERS — THE MORE YOU GATHER TOGETHER, THE MORE BEAUTIFUL THE BOUQUET BECOMES!

MAY 10

BENJAMIN **F**RANKLIN ONCE SAID, "**W**HAT WILL CHANGE YOU MOST IN FIVE YEARS ARE THE PEOPLE YOU MEET AND THE BOOKS THAT YOU READ."

READ A LOT OF BOOKS ON MANY DIFFERENT SUBJECTS, AND MAKE A LOT OF FRIENDS FROM ALL WALKS OF LIFE TO KEEP GROWING AND TO KEEP LIFE INTERESTING. **S**TART TODAY!

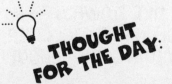

THOUGHT FOR THE DAY: TODAY **I** WILL READ SOMETHING ENJOYABLE FOR AT LEAST HALF AN HOUR!

IMAGINE THAT YOU ARE GOING TO BE ALONE ON AN ISLAND FOR ONE YEAR. YOU CAN TAKE ONLY FIVE THINGS WITH YOU. (FOOD, CLOTHES, AND SHELTER WILL BE PROVIDED.) TELL SOMEONE WHAT FIVE THINGS YOU WOULD TAKE AND WHY.

MAY
11

1.   4.

2.   5.

3.

THOUGHT FOR THE DAY:

SPENDING SOME TIME ALONE HELPS ME TO RECHARGE MYSELF.

MAY 12

PIECE THE FOLLOWING WORDS TOGETHER TO CREATE A POSITIVE THOUGHT FOR THE DAY:

LIVE DAY WILL THIS I HOUR A ONE TIME AT

THOUGHT FOR THE DAY: A GREAT DAY IS MADE UP OF PUTTING EACH HOUR TO GOOD USE!

ANSWER: I WILL LIVE THIS DAY ONE HOUR AT A TIME.

SALLY **R**IDE WAS **A**MERICA'S FIRST WOMAN ASTRONAUT. **W**HEN SHE RETURNED FROM SPACE, SHE SAID, "**I**T'S VERY IMPORTANT TO REALIZE THAT YOU CAN DO ANYTHING YOU WANT TO DO, IF YOU BELIEVE IN YOUR DREAMS AND TALK ABOUT THEM WITH SOMEONE EVERY DAY!"

MAY 13

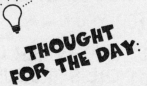

THOUGHT FOR THE DAY: **T**ODAY IS THE DAY TO BEGIN TO MAKE A DREAM COME TRUE!

MAY 14

MOTHER

MOTHERS ARE SPECIAL PEOPLE!
SOME OF US LIVE WITH OUR MOTHERS, AND SOME OF US HAVE OTHER GUARDIANS WHO CARE FOR US. FILL IN EACH LETTER OF THE WORD **MOTHER** WITH A WORD THAT DESCRIBES MOTHER FOR YOU.

THOUGHT FOR THE DAY: THOSE WHO MOTHER US ARE PRICELESS TREASURES IN OUR LIVES.

READ THE FOLLOWING
CHINESE PROVERB:

TALKING DOESN'T COOK THE RICE.

WHAT DO YOU THINK
THIS MEANS?

THOUGHT FOR THE DAY: TAKING ONE ACTION IS
WORTH A THOUSAND WORDS!

MAY 16

ROBERTA WAS AFRAID OF HER ORNERY SCHOOL COACH UNTIL SHE USED ZAP POWER! SHE IMAGINED THAT SHE ZAPPED HER COACH DOWN TO THE SIZE OF A PEA IN HER HAND. IT HELPS HER STAY CALM AND SHRINK HER PROBLEMS DOWN TO SIZE. TRY IT!

THOUGHT FOR THE DAY: WHEN I FEEL STRESSED, I WILL USE MY IMAGINATION TO HELP ME TO STAY RELAXED.

DO YOU HAVE A HOBBY OR A COLLECTION?

MAY
17

IF SO, STAY WITH IT AND KEEP UP THE FUN. IT'S GOOD FOR YOU! IF NOT, TALK TO SOMEONE TODAY ABOUT WHAT HOBBY MIGHT BE OF INTEREST TO YOU, AND ASK THREE PEOPLE YOU KNOW IF THEY HAVE ANY HOBBIES.

THOUGHT FOR THE DAY: HAVING A HOBBY IS INTERESTING AND FUN FOR EVERYONE!

MAY 18

REARRANGE THIS PHRASE ABOUT PEACE. THEN WRITE IT DOWN ON A CARD AND KEEP IT HANDY TO REREAD AND REMEMBER.

THERE ON LET BE AND
PEACE LET EARTH IT
WITH BEGIN ME

THOUGHT FOR THE DAY: MY PEACEFUL THOUGHTS HELP TO CREATE A PEACEFUL WORLD.

ANSWER: LET THERE BE PEACE ON EARTH AND LET IT BEGIN WITH ME.

HERE'S A CREATIVE WAY TO EAT A MEAL OR SNACK TODAY:

MAY 19

FEED SOMEONE, OR LET SOMEONE FEED YOU!
YOU'LL TASTE THE FOOD MORE, LAUGH MORE, AND CHEW YOUR FOOD BETTER!

THOUGHT FOR THE DAY: **A** SHARED MEAL IS A WELL-DIGESTED MEAL.

MAY 20

THINK ABOUT THIS WINNING "TRIPLE-A" QUOTE AND TALK ABOUT WHAT IT MEANS. (LOOK UP THE WORDS IN A DICTIONARY IF YOU NEED TO.)

IT'S YOUR ATTITUDE, NOT YOUR APTITUDE, THAT WILL DETERMINE YOUR ALTITUDE IN LIFE!

THOUGHT FOR THE DAY:

MY ATTITUDE IS THE ONE THING THAT ONLY **I** CAN IMPROVE.

DID YOU KNOW THAT SUCCESS COMES IN A CAN? **T**HAT'S RIGHT— AN "**I** CAN"!

MAY 21

THOUGHT FOR THE DAY: **T**ODAY **I** WILL PRACTICE SAYING "**I** CAN DO IT" OFTEN.

141

MAY 22

BARBRA **S**TREISAND WAS TOLD SHE WOULD NEVER MAKE IT AS AN ENTERTAINER UNLESS SHE HAD SURGERY TO MAKE HER NOSE SMALLER. **S**HE REFUSED, FEELING GOOD ENOUGH JUST THE WAY SHE WAS, AND WENT ON TO BECOME A GREAT SINGER, ACTOR, AND DIRECTOR.

THOUGHT FOR THE DAY: **I**T ISN'T WHAT OTHERS THINK OF US THAT COUNTS, IT'S WHAT WE BELIEVE ABOUT OURSELVES!

WHAT IS THE DIFFERENCE BETWEEN A CHICKEN AND AN EAGLE AS THEY BOTH LOOK UP AT THE SKY?

MAY
23

A CHICKEN LOOKS UP AND SAYS, "NO FLYING TODAY—IT'S PARTLY CLOUDY!"
AN EAGLE LOOKS UP AND SAYS, "IT'S PARTLY SUNNY—ANOTHER DAY TO SOAR!"

MAKE IT A HABIT TO GREET YOUR DAY LIKE AN EAGLE!

THOUGHT FOR THE DAY: I WILL MAKE IT A HABIT TO GO THROUGH MY DAY THINKING LIKE AN EAGLE.

MAY 24

MAYA ANGELOU IS AN AFRICAN-AMERICAN CIVIL RIGHTS LEADER, POET, AND PLAYWRIGHT. HER ADVICE TO CHILDREN EVERYWHERE IS TO "READ EVERYTHING POSSIBLE — LITERATURE THAT'S AFRICAN, AMERICAN, EUROPEAN, LATIN, AND ESPECIALLY, READ SHAKESPEARE."

THOUGHT FOR THE DAY: TODAY I WILL TAKE SOME TIME TO READ SOMETHING NEW.

MAYBE YOU REMEMBER THE ANSWER TO THIS QUESTION FROM AN EARLIER EXERCISE: **W**HAT PERCENTAGE OF OUR FEARS WILL NEVER COME TO PASS?

MAY
25

THE ANSWER IS 95 PERCENT. **T**ODAY, ADD THIS REMINDER WHEN YOU'RE AFRAID: **T**HE OTHER 5 PERCENT WILL HAPPEN ANYWAY, SO WHY WORRY EITHER WAY!

THOUGHT FOR THE DAY: **M**OST OF WHAT **I** FEAR IS JUST THAT — FEAR!

MAY 26

YOU HEAR YOUR FIRST NAME A LOT, BUT DO YOU KNOW WHAT IT MEANS? **I**F NOT, GO TO A LIBRARY AND CHECK IN A BOOK OF NAMES. **LINDA**, FOR EXAMPLE, MEANS "PRETTY" IN **S**PANISH. **JENNIFER** COMES FROM A **W**ELSH WORD MEANING "WHITE SPIRIT." **DONALD** COMES FROM THE **S**COTTISH WORD FOR "WORLD RULER." **C**HECK TO SEE IF YOUR NAME FITS YOUR CHARACTER!

(**I**F YOU CAN'T FIND YOUR NAME LISTED, ASK YOUR PARENTS WHAT YOUR NAME MEANT TO THEM WHEN THEY GAVE IT TO YOU.)

THOUGHT FOR THE DAY: **M**Y NAME IS PART OF WHAT MAKES ME UNIQUE!

FINISH THESE SENTENCES:

PEOPLE ARE IMPORTANT TO ME

BECAUSE _____.

SOMEONE I LEARN A LOT FROM IS

_____.

I LIKE BEING WITH PEOPLE WHEN

_____.

MAY 27

THOUGHT FOR THE DAY:

PEOPLE WHO NEED OTHER PEOPLE ARE THE LUCKIEST PEOPLE IN THE WORLD!

MAY 28

QUICK! THINK OF FIVE THINGS THAT YOU LIKE ABOUT THE WAY YOU LOOK AND WRITE THEM DOWN:

MAKE IT A HABIT TO ZERO IN ON THE THINGS THAT YOU LIKE ABOUT YOUR APPEARANCE WHENEVER YOU LOOK IN THE MIRROR, AND WATCH WHAT HAPPENS TO YOUR SELF-ESTEEM!

1.
2.
3.
4.
5.

THOUGHT FOR THE DAY: WHEN **I** SEE MYSELF IN THE MIRROR, **I** SEE A PERSON **I** LIKE!

LOOK AT THIS CUP OF WATER. IF YOU ARE FEELING OPTIMISTIC, IT LOOKS HALF FULL. IF YOU ARE FEELING PESSIMISTIC, IT LOOKS HALF EMPTY. IT ALL DEPENDS ON YOUR ATTITUDE.

MAY
29

LOOK AT ANY PROBLEMS TODAY FROM THE HALF-FULL SIDE, AND NOTICE WHAT HAPPENS!

THOUGHT FOR THE DAY: TODAY I WILL LOOK AT PROBLEMS FROM THE "HALF-FULL" SIDE AND NOTICE WHAT HAPPENS.

MAY 30

WOULD YOU LIKE TO LEARN A NEW GESTURE TO SHOW AFFECTION?

IN SUMATRA, INSTEAD OF HUGGING, PEOPLE GENTLY PINCH EACH OTHER'S CHEEKS. IN THE MIDDLE EAST AND ITALY, MEN KISS EACH OTHER ON BOTH CHEEKS AS THEY HUG. TRY THESE GESTURES, OR CREATE YOUR OWN GESTURE WITH SOMEONE YOU'RE COMFORTABLE WITH.

THOUGHT FOR THE DAY: OF ALL THE FUN THINGS THERE ARE TO DO, ONE OF THE BEST IS TRYING SOMETHING NEW!

DO YOU PLAY A MUSICAL INSTRUMENT? **I**F SO, PUT EVERYTHING INTO YOUR PRACTICE! **I**F NOT, WHAT INSTRUMENT WOULD YOU LIKE TO PLAY? **F**ILL IN THE BLANKS WITH THREE MUSICAL INSTRUMENTS THAT INTEREST YOU:

MAY
31

1.

2.

3.

WHAT SPECIAL QUALITIES DO THESE INSTRUMENTS HAVE THAT MIGHT SAY SOMETHING ABOUT YOU?

THOUGHT FOR THE DAY: **I** WILL TAKE SOME TIME TO LISTEN TO MUSIC TODAY.

JUNE 1

HERE'S A "MIND-STRETCHING" QUESTION TO ASK SOMEONE TODAY:

WHAT IS GRAYISH-WHITE AND WALNUT-SHAPED, WEIGHS LESS THAN THREE POUNDS, AND CAN OUTSMART ANY COMPUTER ON EARTH?

THOUGHT FOR THE DAY: MY BRAIN IS THE GREATEST INVENTION EVER MADE!

ANSWER: THE HUMAN BRAIN.

UNSCRAMBLE THE FOLLOWING
STATEMENT FROM ALADDIN
TO YOU:

JUNE
2

IN THERE A
IS GENIE ALL
POWERFUL
US OF

THOUGHT
FOR THE DAY:

TODAY I WILL USE MORE
OF MY OWN INNER GENIUS.

ANSWER: THERE IS A POWERFUL GENIE IN ALL OF US.

153

JUNE 3

WALT **D**ISNEY HAD ALREADY FAILED IN THE CARTOON BUSINESS WHEN HE TOOK A TRAIN TO **H**OLLYWOOD, DREAMING OF WORKING IN THE FILM INDUSTRY. **A**T FIRST NO ONE WOULD HIRE HIM, BUT HE HELD ON TO HIS DREAM. **A**ND AS YOU KNOW, HE ULTIMATELY BECAME ONE OF THE MOST SUCCESSFUL MOVIE-MAKERS OF ALL TIME.

WHAT DREAM CAN YOU KEEP ALIVE TODAY?

THOUGHT FOR THE DAY: **T**ODAY **I** WILL IMAGINE IN DETAIL THAT ONE OF MY DREAMS HAS ALREADY COME TRUE!

HERE IS A CHINESE PROVERB
TO THINK ABOUT TODAY:

JUNE
4

IT TAKES THE EYE
OF FAITH TO SEE THE
BEAUTIFUL BUTTERFLY IN
THE CATERPILLAR.

TALK ABOUT WHAT THIS MEANS
WITH SOMEONE TODAY.

THOUGHT
FOR THE DAY:
HAVING FAITH HELPS ME
TO TRUST IN LIFE MORE!

TODAY IS **WORLD ENVIRONMENT DAY**, TO REMIND US THAT IT IS EVERYONE'S RESPONSIBILITY TO TAKE CARE OF THE EARTH. **N**AME THREE WAYS THAT YOU CAN HELP THE ENVIRONMENT NOW:

JUNE 5

1.

2.

3.

THOUGHT FOR THE DAY: **I** AM A WORLD CITIZEN, TAKING PRIDE IN THE WORLD AROUND ME!

USING THE **E-Z** LANGUAGE DECODER ON PAGE 369, DECODE THE FOLLOWING STATEMENT ABOUT LIFE:

JUNE
6

LEZIFE EZIS EZA SEZONG WEZORTH SEZINGEZING; WHEZY DEZON'T YEZOU SEZING EZIT!

THOUGHT FOR THE DAY: **T**ODAY **I** WILL LAUGH AND SING FOR NO REASON AT ALL!

ANSWER: LIFE IS A SONG WORTH SINGING; WHY DON'T YOU SING IT!

157

JUNE 7

WHEN YOU HAVE SOMETHING TO DO, IGNORE THE VOICE THAT TELLS YOU TO DO IT LATER, AND USE **STARTING POWER!** **L**IKE A STALLED CAR, YOU MAY FIND IT HARD TO GET MOVING, BUT ONCE YOU DO, YOU'RE ON YOUR WAY!

THOUGHT FOR THE DAY: **S**TARTING POWER WILL HELP YOU TO MAKE YOUR DREAMS COME TRUE!

PRESIDENT **J**IMMY **C**ARTER ONCE GOOFED IN PUBLIC WHEN HE INTRODUCED FORMER **V**ICE **P**RESIDENT **H**UBERT **H**ORATIO **H**UMPHREY AS "**H**UBERT **H**ORATIO **H**ORNBLOWER." **P**EOPLE LAUGHED, AND SO DID HE. **I**T HELPS WHEN WE CAN LAUGH ABOUT OUR MISTAKES!

JUNE

8

THOUGHT FOR THE DAY: **I**'LL REMEMBER NOT TO TAKE MYSELF SO SERIOUSLY TODAY.

JUNE 9

READ THE WORD PICTURE AND TALK ABOUT WHAT IT MEANS WITH SOMEONE.

MEAL + MEAL + MEAL

a day

THOUGHT FOR THE DAY: TODAY I WILL EAT HEALTHY FOOD TO STAY TRIM AND FIT.

THINK ABOUT
THIS TODAY:

JUNE
10

ONLY THOSE WHO
SEE THE INVISIBLE CAN
DO THE IMPOSSIBLE.

**THOUGHT
FOR THE DAY**:

TODAY **I** WILL BELIEVE
IN SOMETHING THAT **I**
CANNOT YET SEE.

JUNE 11

TRY SAYING THESE TWO STATEMENTS OUT LOUD: "DON'T BE NERVOUS," AND "STAY CALM." DID YOU NOTICE HOW MUCH BETTER YOU FEEL WHEN YOU HEAR THE SECOND SENTENCE? THAT IS BECAUSE IT IS STATED IN THE POSITIVE; IT GIVES YOU A CONSTRUCTIVE ACTION TO TAKE, RATHER THAN TELLING YOU NOT TO DO SOMETHING.

CONCENTRATE ON TALKING TO YOURSELF POSITIVELY TODAY AND EVERY DAY.

THOUGHT FOR THE DAY: TODAY I WILL THINK MORE ABOUT WHAT I LIKE, AND LESS ABOUT WHAT I DON'T LIKE!

TELL SOMEONE TODAY THAT YOU WISH FOR THEM THE THREE BONES OF SUCCESS IN LIFE—THE WISHBONE, THE BACKBONE, AND THE FUNNY BONE:

JUNE 12

ONE FOR DREAMING,
ONE FOR STRENGTH, AND
ONE FOR LAUGHTER.

 **THOUGHT FOR THE DAY:** WHEN **I** DREAM AND WHEN **I** LAUGH, **I** AM STRONG!

163

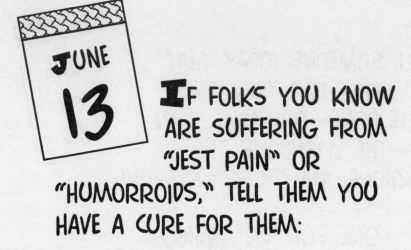

JUNE 13

IF FOLKS YOU KNOW ARE SUFFERING FROM "JEST PAIN" OR "HUMORROIDS," TELL THEM YOU HAVE A CURE FOR THEM:

THOUGHT FOR THE DAY: BECOME "PLAYFOOL" TWO TIMES A DAY AND "GLEEQUILIBRIUM" WILL BE YOURS!

INTERPRET THIS POSITIVE PHRASE, WRITTEN IN THE **N**OUGHTS & **C**ROSSES SECRET CODE.

JUNE

14

(**T**HE KEY IS ON PAGE 367.)

THOUGHT FOR THE DAY: **I** AM CAPABLE OF MORE THAN **I** REALIZE!

ANSWER: YOU CAN DO IT!

JUNE
15

UNSCRAMBLE THE FOLLOWING SIX PHRASES YOU MIGHT USE TO SAY CONGRATULATIONS:

PUSRE OJB

DPLSENID

SBMTUH PU

ZAMAIGN

ERTHE EHCERS

CINE IOGNG

THOUGHT FOR THE DAY:

TODAY **I**'LL GO OUT OF MY WAY TO TELL OTHERS HOW GREAT THEY'RE DOING!

ANSWER: SUPER JOB, THUMBS UP, THREE CHEERS, SPLENDID, AMAZING, NICE GOING.

166

ARE YOU SUFFERING FROM **T**UPPERWARE-BRAIN SYNDROME? **I**T HAPPENS WHEN NOTHING NEW IS GOING INTO THE BRAIN, NOTHING NEW IS COMING OUT OF THE BRAIN, AND IT JUST GETS BURPED FOR AIR EVERY FEW WEEKS! **I**F SO, LEARN SOMETHING NEW TODAY AND START EXERCISING THOSE MENTAL MUSCLES!

JUNE 16

THOUGHT FOR THE DAY: **L**EARNING NEW THINGS GIVES ME ENERGY AND ZEST FOR LIFE!

JUNE 17

DID YOU KNOW THAT CERTAIN WORDS ARE LIKE JUNK FOOD FOR THE MIND? **H**ERE ARE A FEW THAT MIGHT LEAVE INDIGESTION INSIDE— **SHOULD, CAN'T, WON'T, TRY,** AND ALL PUT-DOWNS!

THOUGHT FOR THE DAY: TODAY **I** WILL **F**EED MY BRAIN WITH NOURISHING WORDS, SUCH AS "**I** CAN," "**I** WILL," "**I** BELIEVE," AND ALL COMPLIMENTS!

FATHERS ARE SPECIAL PEOPLE!
SOME OF US LIVE WITH OUR FATHERS,
AND SOME OF US HAVE OTHER GUARDIANS
WHO CARE FOR US. **F**ILL IN EACH LETTER
OF THE WORD **FATHER** WITH A WORD
THAT DESCRIBES FATHER FOR YOU:

JUNE
18

F
A
T
H
E
R

THOUGHT FOR THE DAY: **T**HOSE WHO FATHER US
GIVE US THE GIFTS OF
GUIDANCE, LOVE, AND CARE.

JUNE 19

USE YOUR IMAGINATION TO CREATE YOUR OWN CIRCLE OF EXCELLENCE.

PICTURE YOURSELF STANDING ON A STAGE, SURROUNDED BY A GOLDEN SPOTLIGHT OF EXCELLENCE. YOU CAN STEP INTO THIS CIRCLE WHEN YOU NEED TO RELAX OR FEEL CONFIDENT, SUCH AS BEFORE A TEST, A RACE, OR ANYTHING YOU ARE SCARED ABOUT.

THOUGHT FOR THE DAY: WHEN I CIRCLE MYSELF WITH EXCELLENCE, I GLOW FROM THE INSIDE OUT!

HERE IS A QUESTION THAT WILL SURELY CAUSE YOUR FRIENDS TO DROP THEIR JAWS IN AWE:

IF YOU REMOVED ALL OF THE SPACE FROM FIFTEEN BILLION PEOPLE, AND ONLY THEIR MASS REMAINED, WHAT WOULD THEY FIT INSIDE OF? (**R**EMEMBER, WE ARE ALL 99.9999 PERCENT SPACE!)

JUNE
20

THOUGHT FOR THE DAY: **T**HE UNIVERSE IS FULL OF AWE AND MYSTERY JUST WAITING TO BE DISCOVERED!

ANSWER: ONE SINGLE ASPIRIN TABLET.

171

JUNE 21

INVENT CREATIVE MEANINGS FOR THE FOLLOWING WORDS:

FANTIFFIC

TERRIFICENT

SUPAZING

THOUGHT FOR THE DAY:

TODAY **I** WILL INSPIRE MYSELF BY DOING SOMETHING CREATIVE FOR SOMEONE ELSE.

THIS IS **K**OKOPELLI, THE FLUTE PLAYER. **T**HE **H**OPI **I**NDIANS CREATED THIS FIGURE TO BE A HAPPY MASCOT WHO LEADS FOLLOWERS ON THEIR LIFE JOURNEY.

JUNE
22

CREATE A POSITIVE MASCOT OF YOUR OWN AND DRAW IT IN THE BOX.

THOUGHT FOR THE DAY: **M**Y LIFE JOURNEY IS FULL OF ADVENTURES, FUN, AND CHALLENGES!

173

JUNE
23

HERE IS AN OLD SAYING
ABOUT FRIENDSHIP THAT IS
USEFUL TO REMEMBER:

MAKE NEW FRIENDS,
BUT KEEP THE OLD.
ONE IS SILVER
AND THE OTHER GOLD.

THOUGHT
FOR THE DAY:
BOTH NEW AND OLD FRIENDS
HAVE VALUE IN OUR LIVES!

DECODE THIS POSITIVE STATEMENT THAT IS WRITTEN IN **M**ORSE CODE:

JUNE
24

```
-.--  ---  ..-

.-  .-.  .  .-

.--  ..  -.  -.  .  .-.
```

(**S**EE THE KEY ON PAGE 366.)

THOUGHT FOR THE DAY: **E**ACH STEP **I** TAKE TOWARD A GOAL IS A WINNING STEP.

JUNE 25

WHEN **B**RANDT **L**EGG WAS TEN YEARS OLD, HE BOUGHT A VALUABLE STAMP AT AN AUCTION FOR 75¢ AND LATER SOLD IT FOR $85. **H**E CONTINUED WITH HIS HOBBY, AND BY THE TIME HE WAS SEVENTEEN, HE BOUGHT A $2 MILLION STAMP AUCTION BUSINESS. **H**E SAID THAT HE WAS SUCCESSFUL BECAUSE HE WAS TOO YOUNG TO FEAR THAT IT COULDN'T BE DONE!

THOUGHT FOR THE DAY: **T**ODAY **I** WILL REMEMBER THAT ANYTHING IS POSSIBLE!

LEARN TO "JUST SAY NO" TO PUT-DOWNS!

EVERYONE GETS HURT— ESPECIALLY THE NAME-CALLER! INSTEAD, BUILD PEOPLE UP BY TELLING THEM WHAT YOU APPRECIATE ABOUT THEM. START TODAY, AND WATCH YOUR FRIENDSHIPS GROW!

JUNE 26

THOUGHT FOR THE DAY: TODAY I WILL BUILD OTHERS UP INSTEAD OF PUTTING THEM DOWN.

JUNE 27

DID YOU KNOW THAT THE **L**EANING **T**OWER OF **P**ISA WAS A GIANT MISTAKE? **M**ORE THAN 800 YEARS AGO, THE TOWER WAS BUILT ON UNSTABLE GROUND. **T**HE FOUNDATION BEGAN TO SINK AND THE TOWER BEGAN TO LEAN LONG BEFORE IT WAS FINISHED. **T**HE BUILDERS TRIED TO FIX IT, BUT THEIR EFFORTS ONLY MADE THE TOWER LEAN MORE. **N**OW IT IS A WORLD-FAMOUS TOURIST ATTRACTION!

THOUGHT FOR THE DAY: **S**OMETIMES MISTAKES BRING HIDDEN TREASURES!

DECODE THE THREE WORDS BELOW, WHICH PEOPLE MIGHT USE TO DESCRIBE YOU WHEN YOU ARE LIGHTHEARTED:

JUNE
28

NILOGWG

HRIBGT

HINSIGN

THOUGHT FOR THE DAY: **T**ODAY **I** WILL DANCE THROUGH THE DAY FOOTLOOSE AND FANCY-FREE!

ANSWER: GLOWING, BRIGHT, SHINING.

179

JUNE 29

Twelve-year-old Brian Zimmerman was told that it would be impossible for him to get elected to public office in Crabb River, Texas. Luckily, he didn't believe in the word **IMPOSSIBLE**, and was elected. He became the youngest mayor in the world at twelve!

THOUGHT FOR THE DAY: What was impossible once might be possible today.

EVERYONE NEEDS A SPECIAL SPOT IN NATURE. **I**F YOU DON'T HAVE AN OUTDOOR PLACE THAT YOU CAN GO TO OFTEN, FIND A PICTURE OF A BEAUTIFUL SCENE FROM NATURE, OR INVENT YOUR OWN IN YOUR MIND'S EYE.

VISIT THIS PLACE OFTEN, EITHER IN PERSON OR IN YOUR MIND'S EYE!

JUNE 30

THOUGHT FOR THE DAY: **B**EING OUT IN NATURE HELPS ME TO RELAX AND REJUVENATE!

181

JULY 1

KNOCK KNOCK.
WHO'S THERE?
WEASEL.
WEASEL WHO?
WEASEL WHILE YOU
WORK!

THOUGHT
FOR THE DAY:

I CAN ENJOY THE WORK
I'M GIVEN TO DO TODAY,
INSTEAD OF DREADING IT.

DO YOU HAVE A STRONG WILL OR A STRONG "WON'T"? FAMOUS FOOTBALL COACH VINCE LOMBARDI SAID, "USE YOUR HEART POWER AND LEARN TO SAY 'I WILL' RATHER THAN 'I WON'T.'"

THOUGHT FOR THE DAY: TODAY **I** WILL USE MY HEART POWER AND SAY "**I** WILL!"

DO SOMETHING COMPLETELY UNEXPECTED TODAY.

JULY 3

DRESS DIFFERENTLY, COMB YOUR HAIR IN A NEW STYLE, WEAR A HAT, OR WALK OR TALK DIFFERENTLY! IT WILL KEEP YOU AND YOUR FRIENDS ON YOUR TOES!

THOUGHT FOR THE DAY: SURPRISES PERK UP EVERYONE'S SPIRITS!

TODAY IS JULY 4TH— INDEPENDENCE DAY!

FIND AND CIRCLE SIX WORDS IN THE PUZZLE THAT REPRESENT SIX WAYS WE CAN EXPRESS FREEDOM OF CHOICE.

JULY
4

```
L  W  E  R  O  T
I  O  M  O  E  H
V  R  V  L  A  I
E  K  U  E  R  N
S  P  E  A  K  K
A  L  L  R  E  Z
B  U  A  N  I  O
```

THOUGHT FOR THE DAY: TODAY I WILL CHERISH THE GIFT OF FREEDOM.

JULY 5

WRITE A LETTER TO YOURSELF ABOUT YOUR HOPES AND DREAMS FOR YOUR FUTURE.

SEAL IT, AND PUT IT IN A SAFE PLACE. **G**IVE IT TO YOURSELF ON YOUR BIRTHDAY FIVE YEARS FROM NOW.

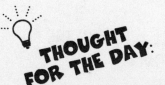

THOUGHT FOR THE DAY: **M**Y HOPE FOR TODAY WILL BUILD MY WORLD OF TOMORROW.

EIGHTEEN-YEAR-OLD VIOLINIST FRANK MAATEN LOST FOUR FINGERS FROM HIS RIGHT HAND—THE ONE HE USED TO PLAY THE VIOLIN. THE DOCTORS TOLD HIM IT WAS IMPOSSIBLE TO PLAY EVER AGAIN. A FEW YEARS LATER, FRANK BECAME THE BEST CONCERT VIOLINIST IN ALL OF SIOUX CITY, IOWA, IN THEIR SYMPHONY ORCHESTRA! TO HIM, THERE WAS NO SUCH WORD AS IMPOSSIBLE.

JULY 6

THOUGHT FOR THE DAY: TODAY I WILL THINK ABOUT SOMETHING I BELIEVED TO BE IMPOSSIBLE AND SEE WHAT HAPPENS WHEN I THINK LIKE FRANK!

JULY 7

WHAT HAPPENS WHEN YOU CROSS A HANDSHAKE AND A BELLY LAUGH?

YOU GET A MIRTHSHAKE!

TRY ANSWERING THE FOLLOWING RIDDLE WITH YOUR OWN IDEA:

WHAT HAPPENS WHEN YOU CROSS A TICKLE AND A HUG?

ANSWER:

THOUGHT FOR THE DAY: **H**UMOR AND PLAY ADD SURPRISE AND FUN TO MY DAY.

188

DID YOU KNOW THAT SOME OF THE WEALTHIEST PEOPLE IN THIS COUNTRY GOT THAT WAY BY LEARNING TO SAVE AND INVEST 10 PERCENT OF THE MONEY THEY EARNED?

JULY
8

TO DO THIS YOURSELF, START TODAY AND PUT $1.00 AWAY INTO A SAVINGS ACCOUNT FOR EVERY $10.00 YOU EARN. **B**EFORE LONG, YOU WILL HAVE A NICE NEST EGG PUT ASIDE.

THOUGHT FOR THE DAY: **I** WILL SAVE TODAY AND REAP THE REWARDS TOMORROW.

JULY 9

SCIENCE-FICTION WRITER STANISLAW LEM HAS A KNACK FOR CREATING UNUSUAL SAYINGS.

HERE ARE A FEW EXAMPLES:

✔ SOMETIMES YOU HAVE TO BE SILENT TO BE HEARD.

✔ A TIRED EXCLAMATION POINT IS A QUESTION MARK.

✔ NEXT TIME, THINK BEFORE YOU THINK.

THOUGHT FOR THE DAY: TODAY I WILL SEE THE USUAL IN UNUSUAL WAYS.

HERE IS A GERMAN PROVERB TO THINK ABOUT TODAY:

JULY 10

WEALTH LOST—
SOMETHING LOST.

HONOR LOST—MUCH LOST.

COURAGE LOST—
ALL LOST.

THOUGHT FOR THE DAY: WHEN **I** RESPECT MYSELF, **I** HAVE INNER WEALTH.

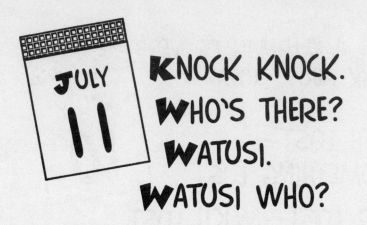

KNOCK KNOCK.
WHO'S THERE?
WATUSI.
WATUSI WHO?

WATUSI IS WHAT YOU GET!

THOUGHT FOR THE DAY: TODAY I WILL REMEMBER TO THINK BIG AND SEE THE BIG PICTURE!

FILL IN THE BLANKS TO MAKE A POEM ABOUT YOURSELF:

JULY 12

I LOVE TO _____.

I WONDER ABOUT _____.

I BELIEVE IN _____.

I HOPE TO _____.

THOUGHT FOR THE DAY: **T**HE GREATEST DISCOVERY OF ALL IS SELF-DISCOVERY!

JULY 13

THIS **N**ATIVE **A**MERICAN SYMBOL IS CALLED **WAKAN TANKA.**

IT MEANS "**T**HE **G**REAT EVERYTHING."

THOUGHT FOR THE DAY:

I AM NEVER ALONE. EVERY PART OF ME IS PART OF **THE GREAT EVERYTHING.**

194

YOUR FUTURE DOESN'T HAVE TO BE LIKE YOUR PAST. **T**HOMAS **J**EFFERSON SAID, "**I** LIKE THE DREAMS OF THE FUTURE BETTER THAN THE HISTORY OF THE PAST."

JULY
14

THOUGHT FOR THE DAY: **I** WILL LOOK AHEAD TODAY RATHER THAN BEHIND ME.

195

JULY 15

SPEND HALF A DAY NOT TALKING AT ALL.

USE GESTURES, FACIAL EXPRESSIONS, OR NOTES INSTEAD.

YOU WILL REALIZE THAT TALKING IS ONLY A SMALL PART OF THE WAY WE COMMUNICATE WITH ONE ANOTHER—SOME SAY ONLY 5 PERCENT! **T**HE OTHER 95 PERCENT IS COMMUNICATED SILENTLY.

THOUGHT FOR THE DAY: **T**ODAY **I** WILL FIND OUT FOR MYSELF WHY SILENCE IS GOLDEN.

YOUR WHOLE BODY FROM HEAD TO TOE IS A MIRACLE-IN-MOTION!

JULY 16

ASK SOMEONE THIS QUESTION TODAY:

HOW OFTEN DOES THE SKIN COMPLETELY REPLACE ITSELF?

THOUGHT FOR THE DAY:

TODAY **I** WILL TAKE THE TIME TO APPRECIATE MY HEALTH AND MY BODY.

ANSWER: ONCE A MONTH.

197

JULY 17

USE THE FOLLOWING WORDS IN A PARAGRAPH TO CREATE A DREAM FOR YOURSELF.

SKY

TRAVEL

SMILES

SOARING

WINNER

TELL IT OUT LOUD TO SOMEONE YOU KNOW TODAY.

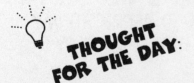

THOUGHT FOR THE DAY: WHEN **I** TALK ABOUT MY WISHES ALOUD, **I** FAN THE FLAMES OF MY DESIRES.

READ THIS CIRCULAR SENTENCE FROM TEACHER **P**ATRICIA **S**UN ABOUT WORLD PEACE:

JULY
18

YOU CAN'T TAKE SIDES•IN A WORLD THAT IS ROUND, YOU

NOW SHARE IT WITH A PERSON YOU HAVEN'T BEEN GETTING ALONG WITH LATELY.

THOUGHT FOR THE DAY: **T**HE NEXT TIME **I** AM IN A CONFLICT, **I** WILL LOOK AT THINGS THROUGH THE OTHER PERSON'S EYES.

199

JULY **19**

Decode the message written in Morse code.

—•— ——— ••—   •— •—•• •

•—•• ——— •••— • —••

(See the key on page 366.)

THOUGHT FOR THE DAY: **I** LOVE YOUS ARE LIKE GOOD NUTRITION — THE MORE WE RECEIVE, THE HEALTHIER WE'LL BE.

ANSWER: YOU ARE LOVED!

200

ON JULY 20, 1969, NEIL ARMSTRONG BECAME THE FIRST ASTRONAUT TO LAND ON THE MOON.

JULY
20

WHEN HE TOOK HIS FIRST STEP, HE SAID,

"THAT'S ONE SMALL STEP FOR A MAN, ONE GIANT LEAP FOR MANKIND."

THINK ABOUT ONE SMALL STEP THAT YOU ARE TAKING NOW THAT MAY BE ONE GIANT LEAP FOR YOUR FUTURE, AND TALK ABOUT IT WITH SOMEONE TODAY.

THOUGHT FOR THE DAY: ONE SMALL STEP TODAY CAN LEAD TO ONE GIANT LEAP AHEAD IN THE FUTURE!

201

JULY 21

HERE IS A THOUGHT TO REMEMBER TODAY AND EVERY DAY ABOUT YOUR FEELINGS:

KNOWING MY REAL FEELINGS BRINGS ME CLOSER TO MYSELF.

THOUGHT FOR THE DAY: **W**HEN **I** SHARE MY REAL FEELINGS, **I** GET CLOSER TO OTHERS.

LOVE IS ONE OF THE GREATEST GIFTS THAT PEOPLE SHARE WORLDWIDE. **H**ERE ARE THREE WAYS TO SAY LOVE IN OTHER LANGUAGES:

JULY
22

FRENCH—**AMOUR** (AH-**MOOR**)
ITALIAN—**AMORE** (AH-**MOR**-AY)
ARABIC—**HOUB** (HOWB)

CAN YOU USE EACH OF THESE IN A SENTENCE SOMETIME TODAY?

THOUGHT FOR THE DAY: LOVE BREAKS DOWN WALLS, OPENS HEARTS, AND KEEPS THE WORLD TURNING.

ASK SOMEONE THIS AMAZING QUESTION TODAY: **H**OW OLD IS THE UNIVERSE?

SINCE THERE ISN'T AN ANNUAL BIRTHDAY CELEBRATION FOR THE BIRTH OF THE UNIVERSE, PICK A DATE AND PLAN A CELEBRATION WITH FRIENDS.

THOUGHT FOR THE DAY: **T**HE UNIVERSE IS A VAST WONDER THAT WE ARE ONLY BEGINNING TO UNDERSTAND!

ANSWER: FIFTEEN BILLION YEARS OLD.

HERE'S A POEM
WRITTEN BY
CHILDREN'S AUTHOR
DR. **S**EUSS.

JULY
24

YOU HAVE BRAINS IN YOUR HEAD.
YOU HAVE FEET IN YOUR SHOES.
YOU CAN STEER YOURSELF
ANY DIRECTION YOU CHOOSE.

> **S**HARE IT WITH SOMEONE YOU
> KNOW WHO NEEDS A LIFT TODAY.

THOUGHT
FOR THE DAY:

WHEN **I** VEER OFF COURSE,
I ALWAYS HAVE THE CHOICE
TO GET BACK ON TRACK!

JULY 25

BE CREATIVE TODAY AND THINK OF AT LEAST TWENTY WAYS TO USE A SHOE BESIDES WEARING IT ON YOUR FOOT.

MANY GREAT IDEAS ARE BORN THIS WAY!

THIS IS CALLED BRAINSTORMING.

THOUGHT FOR THE DAY: **T**ODAY **I** WILL REMEMBER THAT THERE IS MORE THAN ONE WAY TO APPROACH ANYTHING.

206

IN THE ALPHABET, THERE ARE EXACTLY ELEVEN CAPITAL LETTERS THAT HAVE CURVED LINES. **E**XERCISE YOUR MENTAL MUSCLES AND SEE IF YOU CAN COME UP WITH ALL OF THEM IN YOUR MIND'S EYE.

JULY

26

THOUGHT FOR THE DAY:

WHEN **I** LOOK FOR IT, **I** CAN FIND SOMETHING AMAZING IN ORDINARY THINGS.

ANSWER: B, C, D, G, J, O, P, Q, R, S, U

JULY 27

HENRY FORD WAS ABLE TO BUILD MODEL A AND MODEL T CARS AND MAKE THEM AVAILABLE TO EVERYONE, EVEN THOUGH A LOT OF PEOPLE TOLD HIM IT COULDN'T BE DONE.

HE SAID, "WHETHER YOU THINK YOU CAN OR YOU THINK YOU CAN'T . . . YOU'RE RIGHT."

THOUGHT FOR THE DAY: WHENEVER I THINK I CAN, I'M USUALLY RIGHT!

THIS SYMBOL, USED
SINCE ANCIENT TIMES,
STANDS FOR INFINITY.

DRAW THIS SIGN TODAY TO
REMIND YOURSELF THAT YOUR
POTENTIAL IS INFINITE.

THOUGHT FOR THE DAY: **T**ODAY **I** WILL REMIND MYSELF
THAT **I** AM A NO-LIMITS PERSON!

JULY 29

ESPERANTO IS AN INTERNATIONAL LANGUAGE DEVELOPED BY **DR. LUDWIG ZAMENHOF** OF **POLAND**. **HIS** DREAM WAS THAT PEOPLE ALL OVER THE WORLD WOULD SPEAK ONE LANGUAGE. **CAN** YOU GUESS WHAT THIS SENTENCE SAYS IN **ESPERANTO**?

INTELIGENTA PERSONO LERNAS LA LINGVON **ESPERANTO** RAPIDE.

THOUGHT FOR THE DAY: **LEARNING** A NEW LANGUAGE GIVES ME A NEW SKILL AND LOADS OF CONFIDENCE!

ANSWER: INTELLIGENT PEOPLE LEARN THE LANGUAGE ESPERANTO QUICKLY.

SINCE WE USE LESS THAN 5 PERCENT OF OUR BRAIN POTENTIAL, WE ARE ALL GENIUSES - IN - THE - MAKING!

CREATE WORDS FROM THE FOLLOWING LETTERS THAT DESCRIBE TOPICS OR THINGS YOU'RE WILLING TO LEARN MORE ABOUT—STARTING TODAY.

JULY
30

G
E _____
N _____
I _____
U _____
S _____

THOUGHT FOR THE DAY: **T**ODAY **I** WILL TAP INTO MORE OF MY GENIUS POTENTIAL.

211

JULY 31

ASKING "**W**HAT IF?" QUESTIONS IS A GREAT WAY TO STRETCH YOUR MIND TO NEW DIMENSIONS. **H**ERE ARE THREE TO HELP YOU GET STARTED:

✔ **W**HAT IF TIME RAN BACKWARDS?

✔ **W**HAT IF PEOPLE WERE BORN KNOWING ALL THEY'D EVER KNOW?

✔ **W**HAT IF PEOPLE COULD GET AS MUCH MONEY AS THEY WANTED?

THOUGHT FOR THE DAY: **W**HAT IF EVERYONE IN THE WORLD STARTED ASKING "WHAT IF" QUESTIONS?

ANSWER THIS QUESTION:

WHAT DID THE MOUNTAIN SAY TO THE EARTHQUAKE?

AUGUST 1

WHEN TWO PEOPLE FIGHT, THEY BOTH HAVE FEELINGS THAT NEED TO BE HEARD WITHOUT JUDGMENT. BLAMING NEVER SOLVED ANYTHING. THE NEXT TIME YOU ARE IN A FIGHT, SAY, "TELL ME YOUR SIDE OF IT, AND THEN I'LL TELL YOU MINE," RATHER THAN, "IT'S NOT MY FAULT!"

THOUGHT FOR THE DAY: TODAY I WILL REMEMBER THAT THERE ARE AT LEAST TWO SIDES TO EVERYTHING.

ANSWER: IT'S NOT MY FAULT!

213

AUGUST

2

THE NEXT TIME YOU SIGN A LETTER, USE SOME WORDPLAY. HERE ARE A FEW EXAMPLES:

YOURS UNTIL THE OCEAN WAVES,

YOURS UNTIL THE DAY BREAKS,

YOURS UNTIL THE LEMON DROPS,

WRITE YOUR OWN!

THOUGHT FOR THE DAY: TODAY I WILL ENJOY EACH HOUR UNTIL THE SUN SETS!

UNSCRAMBLE THE FOLLOWING SENTENCE THAT YOU MIGHT SAY TO CONGRATULATE SOMEONE:

AUGUST
3

OYU REA STINEDED ROF SRETAGENS!

THOUGHT FOR THE DAY: WHEN **I** COMPLIMENT SOMEONE ELSE, IT GIVES ME A LIFT TOO!

ANSWER: YOU ARE DESTINED FOR GREATNESS!

AUGUST 4

SOMEONE ONCE SAID THAT THE GREATEST GIFT PARENTS CAN GIVE THEIR CHILDREN IS THEIR TIME.

YOU HAVE A RIGHT TO RECEIVE LOTS OF TIME AND ATTENTION. MAKE SURE TO ASK FOR SOME QUALITY TIME TODAY IF YOU FEEL YOU NEED SOME!

THOUGHT FOR THE DAY: IT'S GOOD FOR ME TO LEARN TO ASK FOR WHAT I WANT AND NEED.

216

SOMETIMES, IT TAKES A GREAT IDEA TIME TO CATCH ON.

WHEN **H**ARRY **W**ARNER FIRST HEARD ABOUT THE IDEA OF PUTTING SOUND INTO MOVIES, HE SAID, "**N**EVER. **W**HO THE HECK WANTS TO HEAR ACTORS TALK?" **H**IS BROTHERS TALKED HIM INTO THE IDEA, HOWEVER, AND **W**ARNER **B**ROTHERS BECAME THE FIRST MAJOR STUDIO TO RELEASE A MOVIE WITH SOUND.

AUGUST 5

HAVE YOU HAD AN IDEA YOU'VE LIKED THAT OTHERS HAVE REJECTED? **G**IVE IT ANOTHER CHANCE TODAY!

THOUGHT FOR THE DAY: **T**ODAY **I** WILL GIVE AN IDEA THAT **I** HAVE REJECTED IN THE PAST ANOTHER CHANCE.

AUGUST 6

A SYNONYM IS A WORD THAT MEANS ALMOST THE SAME THING AS ANOTHER WORD. **C**AN YOU COME UP WITH SYNONYMS FOR THESE POSITIVE TRAITS?

EXAMPLE: FUNNY — HUMOROUS, SILLY, HILARIOUS

CARING —

HONEST —

THOUGHT FOR THE DAY: **I** WILL LOOK FOR THE POSITIVE TRAITS IN EVERYONE **I** SEE TODAY.

RECITE THIS SMART TONGUE TWISTER
OUT LOUD:

I'M SENSATIONALLY SMART!
I CAN THINK OF SIX THIN
THINGS AND SIX THICK
THINGS, TOO!

SAY IT THREE TIMES AS FAST AS YOU
CAN TO FLEX YOUR BRAIN BICEPS!

THOUGHT FOR THE DAY: COMING UP WITH NEW IDEAS
KEEPS ME MENTALLY FIT!

AUGUST
8

WRITE A WORD FOR
EACH LETTER OF THE
FOLLOWING WORD:

J _____
O _____
Y _____
F _____
U _____
L _____

THOUGHT
FOR THE DAY:

I'LL CREATE MORE JOY
IN MY LIFE BY SPREADING
MORE AROUND!

HERE ARE A FEW OF YOUR RIGHTS
FROM "THE SILLY BILL OF RIGHTS"
BY DIANE LOOMANS:

1. THE **RIGHT** TO LOUD, UNCONTROLLABLE LAUGHTER.

2. THE **RIGHT** TO FREE TIME FOR DAYDREAMING AND PLAY.

ASSERT YOUR RIGHTS TODAY!

THOUGHT FOR THE DAY: TODAY I'LL ASSERT MY RIGHT TO BE SILLY!

AUGUST 10

ASK THREE "WHAT'S IT LIKE?" QUESTIONS TO SOMEONE TODAY. HERE ARE A FEW EXAMPLES TO HELP YOU GET STARTED:

✔ WHAT'S IT LIKE TO SEE THE WORLD LIKE A CAT?

✔ WHAT'S IT LIKE TO BE THE EYE OF A TORNADO?

✔ WHAT'S IT LIKE TO BE A MOLECULE IN SPACE?

THOUGHT FOR THE DAY: I CAN USUALLY LEARN MORE FROM ASKING QUESTIONS THAN FROM GETTING ANSWERS.

SINCE THE MIDDLE AGES
AUGUST 11 HAS BEEN
KNOWN AS "THE NIGHT OF
THE SHOOTING STARS."

EARLY SKY WATCHERS NOTED AN
ANNUAL METEOR SHOW THAT REGULARLY
PEAKS NEAR THIS DATE.
IT'S A GREAT NIGHT TO MAKE WISHES.

THOUGHT
FOR THE DAY:

TONIGHT I WILL WISH
UPON A STAR BEFORE I
GO TO SLEEP.

AUGUST 12

HERE IS A GREEK
PROVERB TO THINK ABOUT:

NOTHING WILL CONTENT
SOMEONE WHO IS NOT
CONTENT WITH LITTLE.

WHAT DO YOU THINK IT
WAS MEANT TO TEACH?

THOUGHT
FOR THE DAY: I'LL ENJOY THE LITTLE
THINGS IN LIFE.

FILL IN THE BLANKS TO
COMPLETE THIS POSITIVE
AFFIRMATION ABOUT FREEDOM:

AUGUST
13

I _ _ _ _ R _ E
T_ _ E WH_ _
_ A _ T _ O B _ .

THOUGHT
FOR THE DAY:

BEING ABLE TO MAKE CHOICES
FOR MYSELF HELPS ME TO
FEEL GOOD ABOUT MYSELF.

AUGUST 14

INTERPRET THIS POSITIVE PHRASE WRITTEN IN THE **N**OUGHTS & **C**ROSSES SECRET CODE:

LOOK ON PAGE 367 FOR THE **N**OUGHTS & **C**ROSSES KEY.

THOUGHT FOR THE DAY: **I** AM LEARNING TO BE PROUD OF THE THINGS ABOUT ME THAT MAKE ME DIFFERENT FROM OTHERS.

ANSWER: I AM UNIQUE!

226

THE SERENITY PRAYER HAS BECOME ONE OF THE BEST-KNOWN PRAYERS IN THE WORLD.

AUGUST
15

GOD, GRANT ME THE **SERENITY** TO **ACCEPT** THE THINGS **I** CANNOT CHANGE, THE **COURAGE** TO CHANGE THE THINGS **I** CAN, AND THE **WISDOM** TO KNOW THE DIFFERENCE.

IT'S A GOOD ONE TO MEMORIZE AND HAVE READY AT ALL TIMES.

THOUGHT FOR THE DAY: PRAYER AND BLESSINGS HELP ME TO TRUST IN LIFE AND STRENGTHEN MY FAITH.

227

AUGUST 16

WOULD YOU LIKE TO KNOW ONE OF THE GREATEST SECRETS OF SUCCESS?

PLAN AS MUCH OF YOUR DAY AS YOU NEED TO THE NIGHT BEFORE, AND STICK TO YOUR PLAN AS MUCH AS POSSIBLE. YOU WILL HAVE EVEN MORE FREE TIME THAN BEFORE, AND YOU WILL GET A LOT MORE DONE!

THOUGHT FOR THE DAY: HAVING A PLAN DOESN'T HAVE TO BIND ME; IT CAN HELP TO SET ME FREE!

THERE IS AN OLD SAYING,
"ONE PERSON'S HEAVEN IS ANOTHER'S
HELL." EACH COUNTRY HAS CERTAIN
HABITS THAT MAY NOT APPEAL TO YOU,
BUT THAT DOESN'T MAKE THOSE HABITS
GOOD OR BAD, JUST DIFFERENT.
FOR EXAMPLE, IF YOU LIVED IN FRANCE, FROG LEGS
WOULD BE A DELICACY TO EAT! IN SOUTH AMERICA,
MONKEY IS A DELICACY. WHAT IS A FOOD THAT YOU
REALLY ENJOY THAT OTHERS MIGHT THINK IS WEIRD?

AUGUST
17

THOUGHT
FOR THE DAY:

I WILL ENJOY
OTHERS' DIFFERENCES.

AUGUST
18

FILL IN THE
AFFIRMATIONS
USING SIMILES.

I'M AS FREE AS A _____ INSIDE!

I'M AS PEACEFUL AS A _____.

I'M AS ENERGETIC AS A _____.

THOUGHT FOR THE DAY:

TODAY I WILL BE AS CAREFREE AS A CLOWN!

A KARATE MASTER WHO COULD BREAK A BRICK IN TWO WITHOUT BEING HARMED WAS ASKED, "**H**OW DO YOU DO IT?"

SHE SAID, "**I** PUT ALL OF MY MIND AND ALL OF MY ENERGY ON THE GOAL—GETTING TO THE OTHER SIDE OF THE BRICK! **I** NEVER FOCUS ON THE OBSTACLE—THE BRICK ITSELF!"

THOUGHT FOR THE DAY: **I** WILL LEARN TO SEE THE GOAL, RATHER THAN THE OBSTACLE!

AUGUST 20

WE ARE JUST ONE SPECIES IN THIS LARGE COMMUNITY OF LIFE, AND IT'S UP TO US TO CARE FOR AND RESPECT ALL OF THE OTHERS.

ASK SOMEONE THIS AMAZING QUESTION TODAY: HOW MANY ANIMAL SPECIES EXIST ON THE PLANET TODAY, FROM INSECTS TO HUMANS?

THOUGHT FOR THE DAY: I AM PART OF THE EXCITING COMMUNITY OF LIFE!

ANSWER: 10 MILLION!

232

DECODE THE SECRET **E-Z** LANGUAGE TO DISCOVER SOMETHING TRUE ABOUT ALL LIVING THINGS, INCLUDING YOU:

AUGUST
21

EZALL THEZINGS GREZEAT
EZAND SMEZALL EZARE
BEZEAUTEZIFEZUL!

IF YOU NEED HELP, TURN TO PAGE 369 FOR THE **E-Z** LANGUAGE KEY.

THOUGHT FOR THE DAY: TODAY **I** WILL REDISCOVER THE BEAUTY THAT IS ALL AROUND ME!

ANSWER: ALL THINGS GREAT AND SMALL ARE BEAUTIFUL!

AUGUST 22

READ THE FOLLOWING PROVERB BACKWARDS (FROM RIGHT TO LEFT, STARTING AT THE BOTTOM), AND TALK ABOUT WHAT IT MEANS:

UNDERSTAND **I**, DO **I**.
FORGET **I**, HEAR **I**.
REMEMBER **I**, SEE **I**.

THOUGHT FOR THE DAY: SOMETIMES, THE BEST WAY TO LEARN SOMETHING NEW IS TO "JUST DO IT"!

ANSWER: **I** SEE, **I** REMEMBER. **I** HEAR, **I** FORGET. **I** DO, **I** UNDERSTAND.

SHARING YOUR JOYS AND YOUR SORROWS WITH OTHERS WILL HELP YOU TO FEEL SAFE AND WHOLE. **T**ALK TO SOMEONE TODAY ABOUT WHAT THE FOLLOWING SAYING MEANS:

AUGUST 23

> **S**HARED JOY
> IS DOUBLE JOY.
>
> **S**HARED SORROW
> IS HALF SORROW.

THOUGHT FOR THE DAY:

TODAY **I** WILL REMEMBER THAT SHARING MY SORROW IS AS IMPORTANT AS SHARING MY JOY!

AUGUST 24

A YOUNG MAN WON A HORSE AND SAID TO HIS FATHER, "ISN'T IT GREAT?" HIS FATHER SAID, "WE'LL SEE." TWO WEEKS LATER, THE HORSE RAN AWAY. THE SON SAID, "THIS IS AWFUL!" HIS FATHER SAID, "WE'LL SEE." A WEEK LATER, THE HORSE CAME BACK, BRINGING SEVEN VALUABLE STALLIONS. THE SON SAID, "NOW I'M BEGINNING TO SEE."

THE MORAL OF THIS CHINESE LEGEND IS THAT EVENTS AREN'T NECESSARILY GOOD OR BAD, SIMPLY NEW POSSIBILITIES. WHAT SEEMS TO BE GOOD FORTUNE MAY TURN OUT TO BE A DISASTER. AND WHAT SEEMS A DISASTER AT ONE MOMENT MAY LATER TURN OUT TO BE A BLESSING.

THOUGHT FOR THE DAY: THINGS AREN'T ALWAYS WHAT THEY SEEM!

STARE AT YOURSELF FOR A LONG TIME IN THE MIRROR TODAY. **Y**OU WILL SEE A LOVABLE AND CAPABLE PERSON LOOKING BACK AT YOU IN THE MIRROR.

AUGUST
25

LOOK FOR THE GOOD IN YOURSELF, AND OTHERS WILL TOO!

THOUGHT FOR THE DAY: **E**ACH DAY, **I** AM LEARNING TO SEE MY POSITIVE QUALITIES MORE AND MORE.

AUGUST 26

THE ANCIENT VIKINGS USED TO CARVE SYMBOLS INTO STONE.

THIS IS THE SYMBOL FOR **FATHER SKY**. **IT** REPRESENTS COURAGE AND STRENGTH.

THOUGHT FOR THE DAY: **I** AM FULL OF HIDDEN COURAGE AND STRENGTH.

AUGUST
27

WHAT DO YOU GET
WHEN YOU CROSS A BEAR
WITH A STAGE LIGHT?

**THOUGHT
FOR THE DAY:**

I WILL LET MY
LIGHT SHINE TODAY
IN ALL THAT **I** DO!

ANSWER: A LIGHT-BEARER.

AUGUST 28

CHANGE THE LYRICS OF A SONG INTO SOMETHING FUNNY OR MORE POSITIVE TODAY.

HERE'S AN EXAMPLE, WRITTEN BY AUTHORS DIANE LOOMANS AND KAREN KOLBERG:

GLORY, GLORY HUMOR-TO-YA!
GLORY, GLORY HUMOR-TO-YA!
GLORY, GLORY HUMOR-TO-YA!
LAUGHTER IS MARCHING ON!

DO YOU KNOW WHAT THE ORIGINAL SONG WAS?

THOUGHT FOR THE DAY: I WILL BRIGHTEN UP THE DAY TODAY WITH LAUGHTER AND SONG!

ANSWER: "THE BATTLE HYMN OF THE REPUBLIC."

HAVE YOU EVER HAD AN OVERSEAS PEN PAL?

AUGUST
29

IT'S A GREAT WAY TO MAKE A NEW FRIEND AND LEARN MORE ABOUT THE WORLD. YOU CAN ASK AT YOUR LIBRARY TO GET SOME ADDRESSES OF OVERSEAS PEN PAL ORGANIZATIONS AND YOU'LL BE ON YOUR WAY! OR IF YOU PREFER, WRITE A LETTER TODAY TO A FRIEND FAR AWAY.

 THOUGHT FOR THE DAY: HAVING PEN PALS AND FRIENDS FROM AROUND THE WORLD IS EXCITING AND FUN!

AUGUST 30

WINSTON **C**HURCHILL ONCE GAVE A SPEECH TO A GROUP OF GRADUATING SENIORS. **I**T WAS A TOTAL OF NINE WORDS.

HE WALKED TO THE MICROPHONE AND STOOD SILENTLY FOR A LONG TIME. **F**INALLY, HE SAID WITH GREAT PASSION, "**N**EVER GIVE UP. **N**EVER GIVE UP. . . . **N**EVER GIVE UP." **T**HEN HE LEFT THE STAGE.

REMEMBER HIS MESSAGE WHEN SOMETHING'S HARD TO DO TODAY.

THOUGHT FOR THE DAY: **W**HEN SOMETHING IS DIFFICULT TODAY, **I** WILL REMEMBER **C**HURCHILL'S WORDS OF WISDOM.

EVERYONE NEEDS TO BE TOLD NICE THINGS OFTEN!

ONCE THERE WAS A SIX-YEAR-OLD WHO SAID, "MOM, LET'S PLAY DARTS TOGETHER. I'LL THROW THEM AT THE TARGET, AND YOU WATCH AND SAY 'WONDERFUL!'"

YOU MAY HAVE TO ASK FOR THE NICE WORDS YOU NEED TO HEAR. ASK TODAY.

THOUGHT FOR THE DAY: TODAY I AM WILLING TO ASK FOR WHAT I WANT.

243

SEPTEMBER 1

Writer and poet Ralph Waldo Emerson once said,

"For every wall, there is a door."

What do you think he meant?

Look for the doors today!

Thought for the day: If I run up against a wall, I'll look for the door.

244

UNSCRAMBLE THE FOLLOWING SENTENCE ABOUT YOU:

SEPTEMBER 2

WORLD THE
TO YOU
SPECIAL A
ARE GIFT

THOUGHT FOR THE DAY:

TODAY I WILL REMEMBER THAT WHO I AM MAKES A DIFFERENCE!

ANSWER: YOU ARE A SPECIAL GIFT TO THE WORLD.

A MAN FROM INDIA WAS GIVEN A VERY EXPENSIVE FUR COAT FROM HIS FOLLOWERS. EVERYWHERE HE WENT, HE TOOK VERY GOOD CARE OF IT.

BUT ONE DAY, HE LOST HIS COAT IN THE MARKETPLACE. "WE ARE SO SORRY," HIS FOLLOWERS SAID. "DON'T BE," HE REPLIED. "I WAS TIRED OF BABY-SITTING IT!"

SEPTEMBER 3

THOUGHT FOR THE DAY: I CAN ENJOY THINGS WITHOUT GETTING TOO ATTACHED.

DID YOU KNOW THAT THERE ARE 1,440 MINUTES IN A DAY? **T**HAT MEANS THERE ARE 86,400 SECONDS EACH DAY. **C**AN YOU AFFORD TO GIVE FIVE MINUTES (WHICH IS 300 SECONDS) TO THINKING AND PRAYING FOR WORLD PEACE TODAY?

SEPTEMBER

4

THOUGHT FOR THE DAY: **T**ODAY **I** WILL IMAGINE WHAT A PEACEFUL WORLD WILL BE LIKE.

SEPTEMBER 5

Someone once said that there are two buttons we can push to get us started in the morning: the praise button or the panic button.

The praise button says, "Good morning, God," while the panic button says, "Good God, morning again!"

Which one will you choose?

THOUGHT FOR THE DAY: When I wake up today, I will choose the "Good Morning, God" button!

248

A DOCTOR WAS ONCE ASKED, "**W**HAT IS THE BEST WAY TO STAY WELL?"

SEPTEMBER

6

SHE ANSWERED, "**G**IVE FIFTEEN HUGS AWAY EACH DAY!"

THOUGHT FOR THE DAY: **T**ODAY **I**'LL GIVE A LOT OF AFFECTION TO THOSE **I** LOVE AND SEE HOW **I** FEEL AT THE END OF THE DAY.

SEPTEMBER 7

PUT SOME MAGIC IN YOUR THINKING BY ASKING "WHAT IF?" QUESTIONS TODAY.

HERE ARE A FEW EXAMPLES:

✔ WHAT IF MEN COULD HAVE BABIES?

✔ WHAT IF YOUR PARENTS BECAME YOUR CHILDREN?

✔ WHAT IF THE EARTH HAD A TWIN?

THOUGHT FOR THE DAY: WHAT WOULD THE WORLD BE LIKE IF EVERYBODY ASKED "WHAT IF" QUESTIONS?

TODAY IS INTERNATIONAL LITERACY DAY.

SEPTEMBER 8

BEING ABLE TO READ IS A PRIVILEGE! MAKE IT A GOAL TO READ ONE BOOK A MONTH (BESIDES YOUR SCHOOLWORK), AND YOU WILL BE IN THE TOP 2 PERCENT OF READERS IN THE WORLD!

THOUGHT FOR THE DAY: TO READ A BOOK IS TO INVEST IN THE BANK OF KNOWLEDGE.

September 9

Scientist Albert Györgyi said that creative thinking was "Looking at the same thing everybody else sees and thinking something different."

THOUGHT FOR THE DAY: When others see problems, I will see opportunities.

THIS ANCIENT **V**IKING SYMBOL STANDS FOR "THE SELF."

SEPTEMBER
10

IT IS IN BALANCE, CONNECTED, AND STRONG, AND SO ARE YOU INSIDE.

THOUGHT FOR THE DAY:

I WILL SPEND SOME TIME ALONE TODAY GETTING TO KNOW MYSELF MORE.

SEPTEMBER
11

FIND AND CIRCLE THE FIVE SYNONYMS FOR **FRIEND** IN THE FOLLOWING PUZZLE:

```
A    C    O    T    O
L    H    E    A    Z
B    U    E    D    Y
L    M    D    A    K
A    T    E    A    E
P    B    R    O    M
```

THOUGHT FOR THE DAY: **I** AM A FRIEND TO THOSE FROM ALL WALKS OF LIFE.

ASK SOMEONE THIS QUESTION TODAY TO HELP THEM TO GREASE THEIR QUIZZICAL GEARS:

SEPTEMBER
12

WHICH WOULD YOU RATHER BE
— A COMMA, A PERIOD,
   OR AN EXCLAMATION POINT
      — AND WHY?

THOUGHT FOR THE DAY: **I**N MY IMAGINATION, **I** CAN BE ANYTHING **I** WANT TO BE!

SEPTEMBER 13

TWO FROGS FELL INTO A BUCKET OF CREAM. THE FIRST ONE DECIDED TO GIVE UP, AND DROWNED. THE SECOND FROG THRASHED AROUND FOR A LONG TIME TO STAY ALIVE. SOON ITS CHURNING TURNED THE CREAM INTO BUTTER, AND IT WAS ABLE TO PERCH ON THE BUTTER AND JUMP OUT. THE FROG WAS PERSISTENT!

HOW PERSISTENT ARE YOU?

THOUGHT FOR THE DAY: TODAY, INSTEAD OF GIVING UP, I WILL BE PERSISTENT.

EVERYONE HAS A "RISK MUSCLE." YOU KEEP IT IN SHAPE BY TRYING NEW THINGS. WRITE DOWN THREE NEW THINGS YOU HAVE TRIED RECENTLY:

1. _____

2. _____

3. _____

IF YOU AREN'T MAKING ANY MISTAKES, IT MAY BE BECAUSE YOU AREN'T LEARNING ANYTHING NEW!

 THOUGHT FOR THE DAY: MISTAKES ARE JUST RUNGS ON THE LADDER OF LEARNING!

IN JAPAN, TODAY IS RESPECT FOR THE AGED DAY.

SEND A CARD OF APPRECIATION TO A GRANDPARENT OR ELDERLY PERSON YOU KNOW, OR VISIT A RETIREMENT HOME. THE AGING COMMUNITY IS A GOLD MINE OF WISDOM AND EXPERIENCE. HOW CAN YOU TAP INTO IT MORE OFTEN?

THOUGHT FOR THE DAY: THE AGING COMMUNITY IS A GOLD MINE OF WISDOM AND EXPERIENCE.

PLAY THE GAME OF "REPLAY" TODAY WITH YOURSELF OR A FRIEND. WHENEVER YOU SAY SOMETHING NEGATIVE, REPLAY IT WITH YOUR REAL FEELING OR NEED. HERE ARE SOME EXAMPLES:

1. **MY** COUSINS ARE CREEPS. (**I** FEEL SCARED WHEN **I**'M WITH MY COUSINS.)
2. **I** CAN'T STAND **MONDAYS**. (**I** NEED MORE SLEEP **SUNDAY** NIGHTS.)
3. **MY** SISTER IS SLOPPY. (**I** NEED MORE ORDER IN THE HOUSE.)

THOUGHT FOR THE DAY: **TODAY I** WILL REMEMBER THAT UNDERNEATH EVERY NEGATIVE THOUGHT IS A FEELING OR NEED THAT NEEDS TO BE HEARD.

SEPTEMBER 17

DID YOU KNOW THAT GYPSIES HAVE A REPUTATION FOR BEING VERY HEALTHY? ONE REASON MAY BE THAT WHEN THEY ARE SICK, SIX OR EIGHT OTHER GYPSIES SURROUND THEM AND TAKE CARE OF THEM.

WHEN YOU ARE FEELING SAD OR SICK, ASK FOR A LOT OF LOVE AND ATTENTION! IT WILL HELP YOU HEAL FASTER!

THOUGHT FOR THE DAY: WHEN I AM FEELING SAD OR SICK, I WILL ASK FOR A LOT OF LOVE AND ATTENTION!

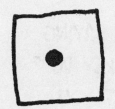

WHAT DOES THIS LOOK LIKE TO YOU?

SEPTEMBER 18

IF YOU ARE LOOKING THROUGH "TUNNEL VISION," IT LOOKS LIKE A PERIOD IN A BOX. **B**UT A GROUP OF FIVE-YEAR-OLDS CAME UP WITH IDEAS SUCH AS A SQUASHED BUG, A COW'S EYE, AND THE TOP OF A NAIL—ALONG WITH FIFTY OTHER IDEAS—IN FIVE MINUTES.

THOUGHT FOR THE DAY: **I** WILL PUT MY IMAGINATION IN HIGH GEAR TODAY AND SEE THE WORLD DIFFERENTLY.

SEPTEMBER 19

HAVE YOU HEARD THE SAYING "MONKEY SEE, MONKEY DO"? WELL, IT'S TRUE. IF YOU WANT TO LEARN SOMETHING FASTER AND BETTER, WATCH SOMEONE WHO IS ALREADY DOING IT, AND IMITATE THAT PERSON. ASK A LOT OF QUESTIONS, TOO!

THOUGHT FOR THE DAY: I CAN LEARN BY FOLLOWING THE EXAMPLE OF PEOPLE I RESPECT.

EVERYBODY FEELS SADNESS AND LOSS SOMETIMES. **H**ERE ARE SOME OF THE FEELINGS WE GO THROUGH WHEN WE LOSE A SPECIAL PERSON, PLACE, OR THING:

SEPTEMBER 20

1. **O**H NO! **I**T CAN'T BE HAPPENING!
2. **M**AYBE **I** CAN DO SOMETHING TO MAKE IT STOP!
3. **I**T IS HAPPENING, AND **I**'M ANGRY!
4. **I** FEEL SAD THAT IT'S HAPPENING.
5. **I**T HAPPENED AND **I** CAN'T CHANGE IT, SO **I** WILL LEARN TO ACCEPT IT AND MOVE ON.

THOUGHT FOR THE DAY: **I** WILL EXPRESS MY GRIEF WHEN **I** LOSE SOMETHING OR SOMEONE.

SEPTEMBER 21

BE A SECRET PAL THIS WEEK AT HOME OR AT SCHOOL.

SURPRISE SOMEONE WITH STICKERS, NOTES, SNACKS, DRAWINGS, OR SMALL GIFTS. **A**T THE END OF THE WEEK, LET YOUR PAL KNOW WHO YOU ARE!

THOUGHT FOR THE DAY:

GIVING SURPRISE GIFTS TO OTHERS WILL BRING ME SOME SURPRISING RESULTS!

264

AN **E**NGLISH PROVERB SAYS THAT ONLY THE WEARER KNOWS WHERE THE SHOE PINCHES. **S**OMETIMES YOU ARE THE ONLY ONE WHO KNOWS SOMETHING HURTS. **T**ALK TO SOMEONE ABOUT WHAT HURTS. **I**T WON'T GO AWAY BY ITSELF!

SEPTEMBER
22

THOUGHT FOR THE DAY: **T**ODAY **I** WILL LET PEOPLE KNOW IF **I'**M HURTING.

THE CHICAGO BEARS HAD TRAINED LONG AND HARD
TO REACH THE **NFL C**HAMPIONSHIP GAME IN 1934.

THE DAY OF THE GAME WAS COLD
AND SNOWY, AND THE PLAYERS HAD
TROUBLE GETTING TRACTION ON THE
FIELD. **A**T HALFTIME, THE **B**EARS LED
THE **N**EW **Y**ORK **G**IANTS 10 TO 3.
BUT DURING THE BREAK, THE
GIANTS SENT OUT FOR SNEAKERS.
THE **G**IANTS WENT ON TO WIN 30 TO 13, AND THE
BEARS SLIPPED AND SLID THEIR WAY TO THEIR
ONLY DEFEAT OF THE SEASON.
THEY LEARNED THAT THE LITTLE THINGS CAN MAKE
ALL THE DIFFERENCE!

THOUGHT
FOR THE DAY:

TODAY **I** WILL PAY
ATTENTION TO THE
SMALL THINGS.

DECODE THE SAYING USING THE SECRET NUMBER CODE.

SEPTEMBER
24

<u>24</u>   <u>11</u> <u>33</u>   <u>11</u>

<u>22</u> <u>15</u> <u>34</u> <u>24</u> <u>51</u> <u>44</u> !

IF YOU NEED HELP, LOOK ON PAGE 368 FOR THE KEY TO THE SECRET NUMBER CODE.

THOUGHT FOR THE DAY: MOST OF US USE LESS THAN 5 PERCENT OF OUR BRAIN POTENTIAL IN OUR LIFETIME!

ANSWER: I AM A GENIUS!

SEPTEMBER
25

SUQUAMISH INDIAN LEADER CHIEF SEATTLE BELIEVED THAT THE EARTH WAS OUR MOST PRECIOUS GIFT. HE IS SAID TO HAVE MADE A SPEECH:

THE EARTH DOES NOT BELONG TO US; WE BELONG TO THE EARTH. ALL THINGS ARE CONNECTED. WE DID NOT WEAVE THE WEB OF LIFE; WE ARE MERELY A STRAND IN IT. WHATEVER WE DO TO THE WEB, WE DO TO OURSELVES.

THOUGHT FOR THE DAY: I WILL HONOR AND APPRECIATE THE EARTH IN ALL THAT I DO TODAY.

Today is World Gratitude Day.

SEPTEMBER 26

Here are three ideas that will help you to develop the gratitude attitude:

1. I AM THANKFUL FOR ALL OF THE GIFTS THAT SOMETIMES GO UNNOTICED—NATURE, SCHOOL, MY BODY, MY HEALTH, MY MIND, AND FREEDOM.

2. I AM THANKFUL FOR THE GIFTS OF LOVE, FRIENDSHIP, FAMILY, AND COMMUNITY.

3. I AM THANKFUL FOR THE GIFTS THAT COME DISGUISED AS CHALLENGES, PROBLEMS, LOSS, OR PAIN.

THOUGHT FOR THE DAY: I WILL MAKE IT A HABIT TO THINK ABOUT ALL THAT I AM THANKFUL FOR BEFORE BED.

SEPTEMBER 27

EVERYBODY LOVES ATTENTION! IF YOU WANT TO MAKE NEW FRIENDS, BECOME A GOOD LISTENER. ASK A LOT OF QUESTIONS TO SHOW YOUR INTEREST IN OTHERS. HERE ARE A FEW TO HELP YOU GET STARTED:

✔ **WHAT IS YOUR FAVORITE TV SHOW OR MOVIE?**

✔ **DO YOU HAVE ANY HOBBIES?**

✔ **WHAT IS ONE OF THE MOST FUN THINGS YOU'VE EVER DONE?**

✔ **DO YOU HAVE ANY PETS?**

THOUGHT FOR THE DAY: WHEN I SHOW INTEREST IN OTHERS, THEY BECOME MORE INTERESTED IN ME!

HERE ARE SOME SYMBOLS THAT PEOPLE SOMETIMES USE IN LETTERS, CARDS, AND STAMPS. **D**O YOU KNOW WHAT THEY MEAN?

SEPTEMBER
28

1. ○
2. ✕
3. ▢
4. △
5. ✳

USE AT LEAST TWO OF THESE WITH A FRIEND TODAY.

THOUGHT FOR THE DAY:

TODAY, **I** WILL CREATE A PERSONAL SYMBOL THAT STANDS FOR ME!

ANSWER: 1. HUGS, 2. KISSES, 3. GIFTS, 4. SPENDING TIME TOGETHER, 5. GIVING COMPLIMENTS

GIVE THIS GIFT OF LOVE CERTIFICATE TO SOMEONE SPECIAL IN YOUR LIFE.

SEPTEMBER
29

This certifies
that

_____

is a very special
person in my life
and is
entitled to

_____ .

This can be
redeemed on

_____ .

THOUGHT FOR THE DAY: I WILL SHOW THE IMPORTANT PEOPLE IN MY LIFE THAT I LOVE THEM TODAY.

SINGER SCOTT KALECHSTEIN WROTE A SONG CALLED "SAY YES TO YOUR DREAMS!" HERE IS A WAY TO SAY YES IN A FEW DIFFERENT LANGUAGES:

SEPTEMBER 30

GERMAN—**JA** (YAH)
RUSSIAN—**DA** (DAH)
JAPANESE—**HAI** (HI)

THOUGHT FOR THE DAY: TODAY **I** WILL SAY **YES** AS OFTEN AS POSSIBLE!

OCTOBER 1

IT HAS BEEN SAID THAT THE ONLY UNCHANGING FACT IN THE UNIVERSE IS THE FACT THAT EVERYTHING IS CONSTANTLY CHANGING. CHANGE IS SOMETHING THAT WILL ALWAYS BE WITH US.

THOUGHT FOR THE DAY: I WILL INVITE CHANGE INTO MY LIFE TODAY!

HERE ARE SOME FUN SYMBOLS TO DECODE:

OCTOBER 2

 IN A

 full

 THOUGHT FOR THE DAY: WHATEVER WE BELIEVE, WE CAN ACHIEVE!

ANSWER: BELIEVE IN A PEACEFUL WORLD.

WHAT HAVE YOU DONE WELL LATELY?
CONGRATULATE YOURSELF BY
GIVING YOURSELF A BIG PAT
ON THE BACK! **N**OW, GO
OUT AND PAT SOMEBODY
ELSE ON THE BACK TODAY!
AND WHILE YOU'RE AT IT,
GO OUT AND EARN ANOTHER PAT
ON THE BACK YOURSELF!

OCTOBER 3

THOUGHT FOR THE DAY: **D**OING MY BEST IS REWARDING AND FUN!

THERE IS AN OLD SUFI MUSLIM TALE ABOUT TWO MEN WHO WENT TO COURT TO SETTLE A FIGHT. THE JUDGE LISTENED TO THE FIRST STORY, AND SAID, "YOU'RE RIGHT." THEN HE LISTENED TO THE SECOND MAN AND SAID, "YOU'RE RIGHT." THE CLERK OF COURT SAID, "WAIT A MINUTE! THEY CAN'T BOTH BE RIGHT!" THE JUDGE REPLIED, "THAT'S RIGHT."

OCTOBER 4

THOUGHT FOR THE DAY:

TODAY I WILL TRY TO SEE THE TRUTH IN THE MANY PERSPECTIVES OF THE PEOPLE AROUND ME.

OCTOBER 5

DID YOU KNOW THAT IF YOU PLACE TWO GUITARS TOGETHER AND PLUCK THE **E** STRING OF ONE GUITAR, THE **E** STRING OF THE OTHER GUITAR WILL BEGIN TO VIBRATE TOO? **T**HIS IS CALLED HARMONIC RESONANCE. **I**T WORKS WITH PEOPLE TOO. **I**F YOU SPEAK FROM YOUR HEART, THE OTHER PERSON'S HEART WILL BEGIN TO COME ALIVE TOO!

THOUGHT FOR THE DAY: **T**ODAY **I** WILL SPEAK FROM MY HEART.

EPICTETUS, A **G**REEK PHILOSOPHER, SAID, "**N**ATURE HAS GIVEN US ONE TONGUE AND TWO EARS, THAT WE MAY HEAR FROM OTHERS TWICE AS MUCH AS WE SPEAK."

THOUGHT FOR THE DAY: **I** WILL LISTEN CAREFULLY TO WHAT OTHERS HAVE TO SAY TODAY.

OCTOBER **7**

WHENEVER YOU SEE YOURSELF IN THE MIRROR TODAY, ZERO IN ON SOMETHING THAT YOU LIKE ABOUT YOURSELF. **W**INK AT YOURSELF AND SAY, "**I** AM COOL, **I**'M OKAY, **I** LOOK BETTER EVERY DAY!" **G**ET INTO THE HABIT OF SEEING YOUR OWN STRONG POINTS, AND OTHERS WILL TOO!

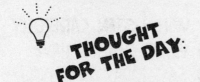

THOUGHT FOR THE DAY:

WHEN **I** FOCUS ON MY STRONG POINTS, OTHERS WILL TOO.

ANNE **F**RANK WROTE, "**W**HOEVER IS HAPPY WILL MAKE OTHERS HAPPY TOO."

OCTOBER
8

THOUGHT FOR THE DAY: **I** WILL DO SOMETHING NICE FOR MYSELF THAT MAKES ME FEEL HAPPY TODAY.

When **D**ick **H**annula, a high school student from **T**acoma, **W**ashington, shattered two swimming records held by **O**lympic gold medalists **M**ike **B**runer and **M**ark **S**pitz,

October **9**

newspaper reporters asked him if he had been nervous. "**N**o," he said, "because **I** had already swum in the race thousands of time in my mind." **H**e was using mental rehearsal. **T**ry it for yourself today. **I**t works!

THOUGHT FOR THE DAY: **T**oday **I** will mentally rehearse for something that **I** want to achieve.

OCTOBER 10

THIS IS AN **E**NGLISH HAND GESTURE FOR PEACE.

MAKE THIS SIGN TO A FRIEND TODAY, OR MAKE UP YOUR OWN GESTURE FOR PEACE!

THOUGHT FOR THE DAY: **E**VERY ACT OF KINDNESS IS A GESTURE OF PEACE.

OCTOBER 11

SOMETIMES SKEPTICS SAY, "**I**'LL BELIEVE IT WHEN **I** SEE IT!" **A**UTHOR **W**AYNE **D**YER WROTE A BOOK CALLED **Y**OU'LL **S**EE **I**T **W**HEN **Y**OU **B**ELIEVE **I**T.

WHAT DO YOU THINK HE MEANT?

THOUGHT FOR THE DAY: **I** BELIEVE THAT TODAY WILL BRING SOME UNEXPECTED SURPRISES!

COLUMBUS MADE A BIG BLUNDER WHEN HE SET OUT TO DISCOVER A FAST ROUTE TO **I**NDIA BY SHIP. **I**T WAS A MISTAKE WHEN HE GOT LOST, BUT HE ENDED UP BLUNDERING HIS WAY INTO A CONTINENT **E**UROPEANS KNEW NOTHING ABOUT— **A**MERICA! **S**OMETIMES MISTAKES LEAD TO DISCOVERY. **S**TOP AND LOOK AT WHAT NEW THING YOU CAN DISCOVER IN ANY MISTAKE YOU MAKE TODAY.

OCTOBER 12

THOUGHT FOR THE DAY:

TODAY **I**'LL REMEMBER THAT SOMETIMES MISTAKES LEAD TO NEW DISCOVERIES.

OCTOBER 13

ABRAHAM LINCOLN ONCE SAID:

"IF I HAD SIX HOURS TO CUT DOWN A TREE, I'D SPEND FOUR SHARPENING THE AX!"

WHAT DO YOU THINK HE MEANT?

THOUGHT FOR THE DAY: I'LL PREPARE MYSELF FOR THE TASKS AHEAD.

DID YOU KNOW THAT THE HUMMINGBIRD IS THE ONLY BIRD IN THE WORLD THAT CAN FLY BACKWARDS, STRAIGHT UP, AND SIDEWAYS?

OCTOBER 14

IT IS THE TINIEST AND BOLDEST BIRD IN THE WORLD. **T**HE HUMMINGBIRD REMINDS US THAT BOLDNESS HAS NOTHING TO DO WITH SIZE!

THOUGHT FOR THE DAY:

I WILL BE BOLD TODAY IN LETTING OTHERS SEE MY STRENGTHS.

OCTOBER 15

YOU ARE A PRECIOUS PERSON WITH SOME BASIC RIGHTS. SAY THESE ALOUD TODAY:

✔ **I** HAVE THE RIGHT TO BE LOVED AND CARED FOR.

✔ **I** HAVE THE RIGHT TO BE HEARD AND UNDERSTOOD.

✔ **I** HAVE THE RIGHT TO SAY NO TO THINGS THAT MAY HARM ME.

THOUGHT FOR THE DAY: **I** HAVE A RIGHT TO EXERCISE MY RIGHTS!

288

HERE'S A JOKE TO PASS ON TO SOMEONE WHO NEEDS A LIFT TODAY.

OCTOBER 16

KNOCK KNOCK.
WHO'S THERE?
MUSTARD BEAN.
MUSTARD BEAN WHO?
MUSTARD BEAN A BEAUTIFUL BABY, CAUSE BABY, LOOK AT YOU NOW!

THOUGHT FOR THE DAY: EVERY KIND WORD I PUT OUT COMES BACK TO ME!

OCTOBER 17

YOU'VE PROBABLY HEARD THE FAIRY TALE "THE UGLY DUCKLING." IT'S ABOUT AN UNUSUAL-LOOKING BIRD WHO IS TEASED BY ALL OF THE OTHER DUCKLINGS FOR BEING DIFFERENT. HE LEAVES THE FLOCK IN SEARCH FOR A PLACE WHERE HE CAN FEEL SAFE. AFTER A LONG SEARCH, HE DISCOVERS THAT HE ISN'T A DUCK AT ALL, BUT A BEAUTIFUL SWAN!

NO MATTER WHAT OTHERS SAY, YOU TOO HAVE YOUR OWN UNIQUE BEAUTY.

THOUGHT FOR THE DAY: TODAY I WILL LOOK FOR MY OWN UNIQUE BEAUTY AND CELEBRATE IT!

FIND AND CIRCLE THE SENTENCE
ABOUT SUCCESS HIDDEN IN THE
FOLLOWING LETTERS:

OCTOBER
18

LCVOGESUCCESSLTUR
THAPPENSLQONENEVD
YDAYLXATLAGMOTIME

THOUGHT
FOR THE DAY:

SUCCESS IS A VENTURE
THAT ALWAYS BEGINS
WITH A VISION.

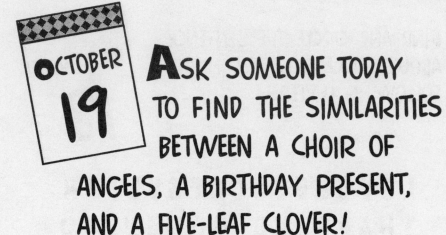

OCTOBER 19

ASK SOMEONE TODAY TO FIND THE SIMILARITIES BETWEEN A CHOIR OF ANGELS, A BIRTHDAY PRESENT, AND A FIVE-LEAF CLOVER!

THOUGHT FOR THE DAY:

TODAY, **I** WILL LOOK FOR THE SIMILARITIES IN MY WORLD, INSTEAD OF THE DIFFERENCES.

STEVEN **J**OBS WAS A DREAMER AND A COMPUTER WHIZ. **E**VERYONE TOLD HIM IT WAS IMPOSSIBLE FOR HIM TO START A COMPUTER BUSINESS AND COMPETE WITH GIANT COMPUTER COMPANIES LIKE **IBM**. **B**UT HE HAD HIS OWN IDEAS ABOUT COMPUTERS AND EVENTUALLY COFOUNDED **A**PPLE **C**OMPUTER, ONE OF THE LARGEST AND MOST SUCCESSFUL COMPUTER COMPANIES IN THE WORLD.

OCTOBER 20

THOUGHT FOR THE DAY: **T**ODAY **I** WILL TAKE A DREAM OF MINE ONE STEP CLOSER TO REALITY.

293

OCTOBER **21** **T**ALK WITH SOMEONE ABOUT WHAT THIS ANCIENT PROVERB MEANS TODAY:

BETTER TO LIGHT ONE CANDLE THAN TO CURSE THE DARKNESS.

THOUGHT FOR THE DAY: **T**ODAY **I** WILL REPLACE MY COMPLAINTS WITH POSITIVE THOUGHTS AND ACTIONS.

A FIRST-GRADER CAME HOME FROM HIS FIRST DAY OF SCHOOL AND SAID TO HIS MOTHER, "MOM, I'M NOT GOING BACK TO SCHOOL AGAIN! I CAN'T READ, I CAN'T WRITE, AND THEY WON'T LET ME TALK, SO WHAT'S THE USE!"

OCTOBER 22

THOUGHT FOR THE DAY: WHEN I AM FEELING DISCOURAGED, I WILL TALK TO SOMEONE I TRUST, GET SOME EXTRA SUPPORT, AND HANG IN THERE!

DID YOU KNOW THAT THE OSTRICH IS EIGHT FEET TALL AND CAN'T FLY? **B**UT THE OSTRICH DOESN'T FEEL "LESS THAN" BECAUSE OF IT! **I**NSTEAD, THE OSTRICH USES ITS LONG LEGS TO RUN AND ITS LONG NECK TO EXPLORE IN THE SAND!

OCTOBER 23

THOUGHT FOR THE DAY:

I WILL LEARN TO BUILD ON MY STRENGTHS AND MINIMIZE MY WEAKNESSES, THE WAY THE OSTRICH DOES!

TODAY IS UNITED NATIONS DAY.

OCTOBER 24

THE UNITED NATIONS WAS CREATED IN 1945 TO HELP PREVENT WAR BY JOINING MANY NATIONS TOGETHER FOR GLOBAL COOPERATION AND CARE. IT HAS BEEN A GREAT TESTIMONY THAT NONE OF US CAN DO ALONE WHAT ALL OF US CAN DO TOGETHER!

WORK TOGETHER WITH OTHERS TODAY TO DO SOMETHING BETTER THAN YOU CAN ALONE.

THOUGHT FOR THE DAY: TODAY I WILL REMEMBER THAT NONE OF US IS AS SMART AS ALL OF US!

THIS IS CLEANER AIR WEEK.

CLEANING UP THE AIR COSTS US BILLIONS OF DOLLARS EACH YEAR. TALK TO SOMEONE THIS WEEK ABOUT WHAT'S BEING DONE IN YOUR COMMUNITY FOR CLEANER AIR, AND LIST THREE WAYS THAT YOU CAN HELP TO KEEP THE AIR CLEAN:

OCTOBER
25

1.

2.

3.

THOUGHT FOR THE DAY: I WILL DO ALL THAT I CAN TO HELP TO CLEAN UP THE ENVIRONMENT TODAY AND EVERY DAY.

DECODE THE FOLLOWING NOUGHTS & CROSSES SENTENCE:

OCTOBER
26

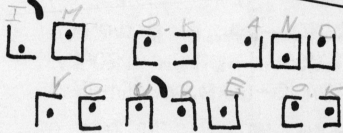

LOOK ON PAGE 367 FOR THE NOUGHTS & CROSSES KEY.

THOUGHT FOR THE DAY:

WE ARE ALL EQUALS INSIDE, NO MATTER WHAT OUR AGE, RACE, OR EDUCATION!

ANSWER: I'M OK AND YOU'RE OK.

OCTOBER 27

FRIENDS ARE SOME OF THE GREATEST TREASURES IN LIFE. **H**ERE ARE A FEW NEW WAYS TO SAY FRIEND:

DUTCH—**VRIEND** (VREEND)
RUSSIAN—**DRUK** (DROOK)
ARABIC—**SADIQ** (SA-DEEK)

USE EACH WITH A FRIEND TODAY, OR BETTER YET, TO MAKE A NEW FRIEND.

THOUGHT FOR THE DAY: **T**ODAY, **I** WILL MAKE A NEW FRIEND OR IMPROVE A FRIENDSHIP THAT **I** ALREADY HAVE.

300

EVERYBODY HAS HUNCHES
SOMETIMES.

A HUNCH IS SOMETIMES
CALLED **INTUITION**.
IF YOU WOULD LIKE TO
PLAY AN INTUITION GAME, PUT
SOMETHING IN A SHOE BOX. **T**ELL A FRIEND TO
USE INTUITION TO GUESS WHAT'S IN THE BOX.
ANSWER ANY QUESTIONS ONLY WITH YES OR
NO ANSWERS. **Y**OU MAY BE SURPRISED HOW
QUICKLY YOUR FRIEND GUESSES THE ANSWER!

**THOUGHT
FOR THE DAY**: **I** CAN TRUST
MY INTUITION.

OCTOBER
28

OCTOBER
29

HERE IS A TONGUE TWISTER TO SAY AS FAST AS YOU CAN:

I THOUGHT A THOUGHT, BUT THE THOUGHT I THOUGHT I THOUGHT, WASN'T THE THOUGHT I THOUGHT. IF THE THOUGHT I THOUGHT I THOUGHT HAD BEEN THE THOUGHT I THOUGHT I THOUGHT, I WOULDN'T HAVE TO THINK SO MUCH!

THOUGHT FOR THE DAY:

SOMETIMES IT'S BEST JUST TO ENJOY LIFE INSTEAD OF TRYING TO FIGURE IT OUT.

302

WRITE THIS PHRASE ON A BLACKBOARD OR A PIECE OF PAPER TODAY AND SEE IF ANYONE FIGURES IT OUT:

OCTOBER 30

WHIRLED PEAS 4EVER!

(HINT: **I**T IS THE WORLD'S GREATEST DREAM.)

THOUGHT FOR THE DAY:

EVERY GOOD WISH THAT **I** HAVE PLANTS A SEED OF HOPE INTO THE WORLD.

ANSWER: WORLD PEACE FOREVER!

TODAY IS HALLOWEEN —
A GREAT DAY TO DECK OUT
AND LET YOUR CREATIVE,
WILD SIDE OUT TO PLAY!

DO SOMETHING UNUSUAL TODAY,
BESIDES WEARING A COSTUME.
EVERYBODY LOVES THE UNEXPECTED.

THOUGHT FOR THE DAY: TODAY **I** WILL KEEP IN
MIND THAT EVERYBODY
LOVES THE UNEXPECTED!

TODAY IS AUTHORS DAY!

NOVEMBER 1

THANKS TO THE MILLIONS OF WRITERS THE WORLD OVER, WE ARE BLESSED WITH BOOKS AND KNOWLEDGE.

LIST THREE OF YOUR FAVORITE AUTHORS BELOW:

1.
2.
3.

IF YOU ENJOY WRITING, KEEP A DAILY DIARY OR JOURNAL. THERE MAY BE A BOOK IN YOU WAITING TO COME OUT!

THOUGHT FOR THE DAY: A GOOD BOOK IS FOOD FOR THE BRAIN.

NOVEMBER
2

CREATE A SILLY MOTTO TO
LIGHTEN YOUR DAY TODAY.
HERE ARE TWO EXAMPLES:

THE **N**ORTH **W**IND SAYS,
"**B**REEZY COME, BREEZY GO."
A 747'S MOTTO IS,
"**I**F AT FIRST YOU DON'T SUCCEED,
FLY, FLY AGAIN!"

YOUR MOTTO:

THOUGHT FOR THE DAY: **L**EARNING MOTTOES
HELPS ME TO STAY ON
A POSITIVE TRACK!

ANSWER THIS QUESTION:

HOW DO ANGELS GREET ONE ANOTHER EACH DAY?

NOVEMBER
3

THOUGHT FOR THE DAY: TODAY I WILL BE AN ANGEL TO OTHERS BY SMILING AND BEING FRIENDLY!

ANSWER: THEY SMILE AND WAVE HALO!

NOVEMBER 4

TWO TOADS IN A HAMMOCK
READY TO KISS,
WHEN ALL OF A SUDDEN
IT GOES LIKE ¡**SIHT**

SOMETIMES THE UNEXPECTED
SHOWS UP. **W**HEN IT DOES,
LOOK FOR THE HUMOR IN IT!

THOUGHT FOR THE DAY: **T**ODAY **I** WILL WELCOME
THE UNEXPECTED!

UNSCRAMBLE THE FOLLOWING WORDS THAT YOU MIGHT SAY WHEN YOU ARE INSPIRED:

NOVEMBER
5

FIRETRIC
LOFEWUNDR
CISTTAFAN
SEMAWOE

THOUGHT FOR THE DAY:

TODAY **I** WILL THINK ABOUT WHAT INSPIRES ME, AND HOW **I** CAN DO IT MORE OFTEN!

ANSWER: TERRIFIC, WONDERFUL, FANTASTIC, AWESOME

SOMEONE ONCE SAID, "WHEN SUCCESS GOES TO SOMEONE'S HEAD, IT GENERALLY FINDS NOTHING THERE."

NOVEMBER 6

WHAT DO YOU THINK THIS MEANS? ASK SOMEONE TO HELP YOU IF YOU NEED IT.

THOUGHT FOR THE DAY: I CAN ENJOY MY SUCCESSES.

DECORATE YOUR HOUSE WITH SOMETHING SPECIAL THIS WEEK—FLOWERS, A NEW PICTURE, OR YOUR OWN WORK OF ART— TO CELEBRATE YOUR DWELLING PLACE!

IF YOU LIVED IN SOME OTHER PARTS OF THE WORLD, YOU MIGHT LIVE IN A DIFFERENT SHELTER:

NOVEMBER 7

TURKEY—CLIFF DWELLINGS
ALASKA—IGLOOS
ARABIA—TENTS
NEW **G**UINEA—HUTS

THOUGHT FOR THE DAY: **I** TAKE PRIDE IN THE PLACE WHERE **I** LIVE BY KEEPING IT NEAT AND CLEAN.

311

HERE ARE SOME FUN SYMBOLS TO DECODE:

U-R-A -Ful

NOVEMBER 8

 THOUGHT FOR THE DAY:

TODAY I WILL GO OUT OF MY WAY TO GIVE SOMEONE ELSE A COMPLIMENT.

ANSWER: YOU ARE A WONDERFUL PERSON!

THERE IS AN OLD FABLE FROM THE MIDDLE EAST ABOUT A PRISONER WHO WAS SENTENCED TO DEATH. THE PERSIAN KING GAVE HIM A CHOICE—A QUICK DEATH BY FIRING SQUAD, OR A WALK THROUGH A MYSTERIOUS BLACK DOOR. THE PRISONER CHOSE THE QUICK DEATH AND THEN ASKED WHAT WAS BEHIND THE BLACK DOOR. "FREEDOM," THE KING REPLIED, "BUT FEW PEOPLE ARE BRAVE ENOUGH TO FACE THE UNKNOWN."

NOVEMBER 9

THOUGHT FOR THE DAY: I WILL TRY BEING MORE COURAGEOUS THE NEXT TIME I FACE THE UNKNOWN!

NOVEMBER 10

A JOURNEY OF A THOUSAND MILES MUST BEGIN WITH A SINGLE STEP.

TO READ THIS "BACKWARD SENTENCE" WRITTEN OVER 2500 YEARS AGO BY **C**HINESE PHILOSOPHER **L**AO-TZU (LOUD-ZOO), HOLD THIS PAGE UP TO A MIRROR.

THOUGHT FOR THE DAY: **T**HE MOST COURAGEOUS STEP OF ALL IS THE STEP AWAY FROM FEAR AND TOWARD A GOAL!

HAVE SOME PUN FUN TODAY. ASK SOMEONE, "WHAT IS 5Q + 5Q?" WHEN THEY ANSWER "10Q," YOU SAY, "YOU'RE WELCOME!"

NOVEMBER 11

(THIS PUN IS ALSO A REMINDER THAT EVERYONE LOVES TO BE TOLD "10Q" OFTEN!)

THOUGHT FOR THE DAY:

I WILL SPRINKLE MY DAY WITH SOME "PUN FUN" TODAY!

NOVEMBER 12

DID YOU KNOW THAT THE **E**ARTH IS ABOUT FORTY-SIX MILLION YEARS OLD, AND THAT HUMANS HAVE BEEN LIVING ON THE **E**ARTH FOR ONLY ABOUT TWO MILLION YEARS. **T**HIS MEANS THAT IF THE HISTORY OF THE EARTH COULD BE SPACED OVER A DAY, HUMANS WOULDN'T ARRIVE ON THE SCENE UNTIL NEARLY 11:00 P.M.!

THOUGHT FOR THE DAY: **M**Y TROUBLES AREN'T SO IMPORTANT SOMETIMES IF **I** TAKE TIME TO SEE THE "BIG PICTURE."

WHAT HAPPENS WHEN YOU CROSS **A**LBERT **E**INSTEIN WITH A SLEEPWALKER?

NOVEMBER

13

(**T**HE REAL MESSAGE OF THIS JOKE IS THAT WHEN YOU GET THE SLEEP YOU NEED EACH NIGHT, YOU WILL IMPROVE YOUR STUDY HABITS!)

THOUGHT FOR THE DAY:

WHEN **I** GET ENOUGH **ZZZ**'S, THE DAY'S TASKS BECOME A BREEZE!

ANSWER: **Y**OU GET A'S WHILE YOU ARE GETTING **ZZZ**'S!

317

NOVEMBER 14

HERE IS A "TREE-MENDOUS" QUOTE TO SHARE WITH SOMEONE:

HIDDEN IN
EACH ACORN
IS A MIGHTY OAK.

THOUGHT FOR THE DAY: **S**EEDS OF GREATNESS LIE HIDDEN IN ME.

ARE YOU FEELING OVERWORKED AND "UNDERPLAYED"? **S**OMETIMES STRESS, HOMEWORK, OR OTHER CHALLENGES IN OUR LIVES DISTRACT US, AND WE FORGET TO PLAY AND HAVE FUN! **I**F THAT'S TRUE FOR YOU, PLAN FOR A LONG PLAY BREAK THIS WEEK, AND DO SOME "INTERNAL JOGGING" BY LAUGHING A LOT! (**I**F YOU'RE "OVERPLAYED" AND UNDERWORKED, STRENGTHEN YOUR HOUSEWORK MUSCLES INSTEAD!)

THOUGHT FOR THE DAY: A BALANCE OF WORK AND A BALANCE OF PLAY IS WHAT MAKES A HAPPY, PRODUCTIVE DAY!

NOVEMBER 15

A WISE WOMAN ASKED A YOUNG GIRL, "WHAT THREE WORDS DO HUMANS USE MORE THAN ANY OTHERS?"

SHE ANSWERED, "I DON'T KNOW."

THE WISE WOMAN RESPONDED, "THAT'S RIGHT!"

NOVEMBER 16

THE NEXT TIME YOU HEAR YOURSELF SAY, "I DON'T KNOW," ASK YOURSELF, "IF I DID KNOW, WHAT WOULD THE ANSWER BE?" AND WATCH WHAT HAPPENS!

THOUGHT FOR THE DAY: I HAVE MORE ANSWERS THAN I REALIZE.

DECODE THE FOLLOWING AFFIRMATION IN MORSE CODE:

NOVEMBER 17

●—●●   ●●   ●●—●   ●

●●   ●●●   ●—

——●   ●●   ●●—●   —

SEE PAGE 366 FOR THE CODE.

THOUGHT FOR THE DAY: IT'S EASY TO FORGET THAT IT'S A PRIVILEGE JUST TO BE ALIVE. TODAY I WILL REMEMBER!

ANSWER: LIFE IS A GIFT.

321

NOVEMBER 18

DO YOU EVER PLAN TO DO ABSOLUTELY NOTHING? **IT** CAN BE GOOD FOR YOUR HEALTH AND YOU CAN DO IT ANYWHERE. **T**AKE AN HOUR TODAY TO DO ABSOLUTELY NOTHING.

THOUGHT FOR THE DAY: **T**HERE IS SOMETHING WONDERFUL TO BE SAID ABOUT DOING ABSOLUTELY NOTHING!

WHAT DO YOU SEE IN THIS PICTURE? A LIGHTBULB, OR AN ELEPHANT ON A STOOL?

NOVEMBER
19

THOUGHT FOR THE DAY: **I** WILL KEEP IN MIND TODAY THAT THERE IS USUALLY MORE THAN ONE WAY TO LOOK AT A SITUATION!

NOVEMBER
20

CREATE A THANK-YOU BLOCK LETTER FOR SOMEONE YOU WANT TO EXPRESS APPRECIATION TO.
HERE IS AN EXAMPLE:

THOUGHT FOR THE DAY: WHEN I EXPRESS APPRECIATION TO SOMEONE ELSE, IT ALWAYS COMES BACK TO ME!

CREATE SOME FICTITIOUS (MADE-UP) FUN-PUN BOOK TITLES TO KEEP YOUR SPIRITS UP TODAY. HERE ARE A FEW EXAMPLES:

NOVEMBER 21

HOW TO APOLOGIZE, BY THAY R. THORRY

EAT YOUR BREAKFAST, BY HAMMOND EGGS

WILL YOU OR WON'T YOU? BY MAE B. SEW

_____ BY _____

_____ BY _____

THOUGHT FOR THE DAY: CREATIVE THINKING KEEPS ME FEELING ALIVE, AWAKE, AND ALERT!

NOVEMBER
22

HERE'S A POPULAR SAYING TO THINK ABOUT AND TALK TO SOMEONE ABOUT TODAY:

KEEP YOUR WORDS SOFT AND SWEET, FOR YOU NEVER KNOW WHEN YOU'LL HAVE TO EAT THEM!

THOUGHT FOR THE DAY:

TODAY **I** WILL TREAT OTHERS THE WAY **I** WANT TO BE TREATED MYSELF.

THERE ARE MANY DIFFERENT RELIGIONS IN THE WORLD, AND ALL OF THEM HAVE SOMETHING TO TEACH US. HERE ARE A FEW CLUES FOR THE FOUR MOST COMMON ONES:

NOVEMBER 23

1. C - - - - T - - N   1833 MILLION
2. M - - L - -   971 MILLION
3. H - - D -   733 MILLION
4. B - - - H - - T   315 MILLION

PICK ONE THAT ISN'T YOURS AND LEARN MORE ABOUT IT TODAY.

THOUGHT FOR THE DAY:

I WILL LEARN SOMETHING INTERESTING ABOUT A NEW RELIGION TODAY.

DID YOU KNOW THAT HONEYBEES VISIT 50 TO 100 FLOWERS DURING ONE COLLECTION TRIP?

EVEN MORE AMAZING, HONEYBEES MUST TAP TWO MILLION FLOWERS TO MAKE ONE POUND OF HONEY!

WHEN YOU HAVE A BIG JOB TO DO, REMEMBER TO TAKE IT ONE STEP AT A TIME, AND GET A LOT OF SUPPORT AND ENCOURAGEMENT ALONG THE WAY.

NOVEMBER 24

LIKE THE HONEYBEE, OVER TIME YOU'LL AMAZE YOURSELF!

THOUGHT FOR THE DAY: **E**VERY LONG JOURNEY IS MADE UP OF MANY SMALL STEPS.

HERE'S A FUN WAY TO LET
SOMEONE IN YOUR FAMILY
KNOW YOU CARE:

NOVEMBER 25

KNOCK KNOCK.
WHO'S THERE?
REVEREND.
REVEREND WHO?
REVEREND EVER—THAT'S
HOW LONG I'LL LOVE YOU!

THOUGHT FOR THE DAY: MOST OF THE IMPORTANT
THINGS WE DO IN LIFE, WE
DO TO GIVE OR RECEIVE LOVE!

A CENTIPEDE WAS QUITE HAPPY
UNTIL A SPIDER IN FUN
SAID, "HEY, WHICH LEG
COMES AFTER WHICH?"
THIS RAISED HER MIND
TO SUCH A PITCH,
SHE LAY DISTRACTED IN THE DITCH,
PONDERING HOW TO RUN!

THE MORAL: THINKING A TASK OUT HAS
ITS PLACE, BUT THERE COMES A TIME
WHEN YOU HAVE TO JUST DO IT!

THOUGHT FOR THE DAY: SOMETIMES IT WORKS
BEST TO ACT, RATHER
THAN TO THINK.

HERE ARE A COUPLE OF EXAMPLES OF
USING IDIOMS TO PUMP YOURSELF UP.

I AM SOARING TO NEW
HEIGHTS IN MY LIFE!
MY OWN POTENTIAL REALLY
BLOWS MY MIND!

NOW, FILL IN THE BLANK TO REMIND YOURSELF OF
WHAT YOUR FRIENDS WILL ENJOY ABOUT YOU TODAY.

_____ **T**ICKLES **T**HEIR **F**ANCY!

THINKING POSITIVELY
REALLY REVS MY ENGINE!

NOVEMBER 28

HERE ARE A FEW THOUGHTS THAT ARE LIKE WEEDS TO PULL FROM THE GARDEN OF YOUR MIND WHENEVER THEY CROP UP TODAY (OR ANY DAY!).

- ✔ **I** HAVE TO DO EVERYTHING MYSELF AND SHOULDN'T ASK FOR HELP.
- ✔ **IT'S** NOT **OK** TO CRY OR SHOW MY FEELINGS.
- ✔ **O**THER PEOPLE ALWAYS KNOW WHAT'S BEST FOR ME.
- ✔ **I** CAN'T TALK ABOUT MY PROBLEM—NOBODY WILL UNDERSTAND.

THOUGHT FOR THE DAY:

TODAY I WILL PULL A MENTAL WEED AND PLANT A GOOD SEED.

PUT THE LETTERS IN THE BOX
TOGETHER TO SPELL A WORD THAT
STARTS WITH AN "M" AND
DESCRIBES YOU ALL THE WAY!

NOVEMBER
29

THOUGHT FOR THE DAY:

TODAY I WILL REMIND MYSELF
THAT I AM A MARVEL!

NOVEMBER

30

DECODE THIS POSITIVE AFFIRMATION FROM THE **E-Z S**ECRET LANGUAGE.

EZI EZAM EZA SHEZINEZING STEZAR!

SEE PAGE 369 FOR THE CODE.

THOUGHT FOR THE DAY: **T**ODAY **I** WILL LET THE BRIGHT LIGHT WITHIN ME SHINE FORTH.

ANSWER: **I** AM A SHINING STAR!

334

THE PEACE SIGN HAS BECOME ONE OF THE MOST POPULAR SYMBOLS IN THE WORLD! **H**ERE ARE A FEW NEW WAYS TO SAY PEACE:

DECEMBER
1

HEBREW—SHALOM (SHAH-LOWM)
SPANISH—PAZ (PAHS)
GREEK—IRI'NI (AH-REEN NEE)

SEE IF YOU CAN USE ALL THREE TODAY WITH DIFFERENT FRIENDS.

THOUGHT **FOR THE DAY**:

THERE IS AT LEAST ONE WORD FOR PEACE IN EVERY LANGUAGE. **T**ODAY **I** WILL LEARN A FEW OF THEM.

DECEMBER 2

HERE IS A GREAT IDEA TO MEMORIZE THAT WILL HELP YOU GIVE SELF-ESTEEM TO OTHERS.

THOUGHT FOR THE DAY: TODAY **I** WILL REACH OUT IN A SPECIAL WAY. TODAY **I** WILL GIVE **TEN** COMPLIMENTS AWAY!

AT THE 1984 **O**LYMPIC **G**AMES IN **L**OS **A**NGELES, SIXTEEN-YEAR-OLD GYMNAST **M**ARY **L**OU **R**ETTON CAPTURED THE HEARTS OF MILLIONS OF PEOPLE WITH HER SUCCESSFUL PERFORMANCES. **S**HE SAID SHE HAD BEEN IMAGINING HERSELF PERFORMING WITH SUPER CONFIDENCE FOR MONTHS—OVER AND OVER AGAIN.

DECEMBER

3

THOUGHT FOR THE DAY: **W**HEN **I** WANT TO SUCCEED AT SOMETHING, **I** WILL SEE IT HAPPENING OVER AND OVER IN MY MIND THE WAY **M**ARY **L**OU DID!

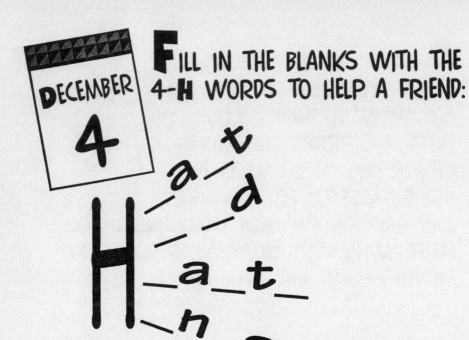

FILL IN THE BLANKS WITH THE 4-**H** WORDS TO HELP A FRIEND:

DECEMBER

4

H_a_t

___a___d

H_a_t_

__n_s

THOUGHT FOR THE DAY:

I WILL REACH OUT TO HELP A FRIEND TODAY FOR NO REASON AT ALL!

ANSWER: HEART, HEAD, HEALTH, AND HANDS.

338

AN OXYMORON IS AN EXPRESSION THAT PUTS TWO OPPOSITE IDEAS TOGETHER TO CREATE AN UNUSUAL PHRASE.

DECEMBER 5

HERE ARE A FEW EXAMPLES: WHISPERING LOUDLY
OUTRAGEOUSLY SUBTLE
THINKING OUT LOUD

NOW MAKE YOUR OWN TO DESCRIBE A SPECIAL QUALITY OF YOURS THAT YOU'LL MAKE A POINT TO SHARE TODAY.

THOUGHT FOR THE DAY:

TODAY **I** WILL HAVE A "WILDLY CALM" DAY!

339

FILL IN THE BLANKS TO CREATE A SENTENCE ABOUT HOW TO LOVE PEOPLE MORE:

I CE--B--T- T-E
D-F-E--N--S -N
E-E-YB-D-!

THOUGHT FOR THE DAY: IF ALL OF MY FRIENDS WERE JUST LIKE ME, THERE WOULDN'T BE MUCH TO LEARN FROM THEM. VARIETY IS THE SPICE OF FRIENDSHIP.

ANSWER: I CELEBRATE THE DIFFERENCES IN EVERYBODY!

COMPLETE THE FOLLOWING STATEMENTS
BY CHECKING THE BOXES:

	ALWAYS	SOMETIMES	RARELY
1. I GET ENOUGH TIME TO RELAX.	☐	☐	☐
2. I SEE MY FRIENDS OUTSIDE OF SCHOOL OFTEN.	☐	☐	☐
3. I TAKE PART IN A HOBBY I ENJOY.	☐	☐	☐
4. I LAUGH OFTEN DURING THE DAY.	☐	☐	☐

IF YOU HAVE CHECKED ANY OF
THE "RARELY" BOXES, TALK TO
SOMEONE ABOUT HOW TO RELAX
MORE AND HAVE MORE FUN!

DECEMBER
7

THOUGHT FOR THE DAY: ABOVE ALL
ELSE, LIFE IS MEANT
TO BE ENJOYED!

341

DECEMBER 8

NOVELIST EDITH WHARTON WROTE, "THERE ARE TWO WAYS OF SPREADING LIGHT: TO BE THE CANDLE OR THE MIRROR THAT REFLECTS IT."

TALK TO SOMEONE TODAY ABOUT WHAT YOU THINK THIS MEANS.

THOUGHT FOR THE DAY: WHEN **I** CAN SEE SOMEONE ELSE'S INNER LIGHT, IT BRIGHTENS MY OWN!

A HINK-PINK IS A RHYMING PHRASE THAT DESCRIBES SOMETHING NICE ABOUT YOU. HERE ARE A COUPLE OF EXAMPLES:

DECEMBER 9

PRETTY AND WITTY
   MILES OF SMILES

CREATE YOUR OWN HINK-PINK BELOW.

THOUGHT FOR THE DAY:

TODAY I WILL CREATE A DAY THAT IS "COMPLETELY NEAT"!

DECEMBER
10

DECODE THE FOLLOWING POSITIVE STATEMENT FROM THE **S**ECRET **N**UMBER LANGUAGE.

24 11 33   33   55   35 53 34
___ ___ ___   ___   ___   ___ ___ ___

12 15 44 45   21 43 24 15 34 14
___ ___ ___ ___   ___ ___ ___ ___ ___ ___

(**T**HE KEY IS ON PAGE 368.)

THOUGHT FOR THE DAY: **T**HROUGHOUT MY LIFE, THERE IS ONE PERSON WHO WILL NEVER LEAVE MY SIDE — **ME!**

ANSWER: I AM MY OWN BEST FRIEND!

IN THE AMAZON JUNGLE, THERE ARE 900 DIFFERENT SPECIES OF WASPS, EACH OF WHICH POLLINATES A DIFFERENT FIG TREE. THESE FIG TREES ARE THE MAIN SOURCE OF FOOD FOR THE SMALL MAMMALS OF THE FOREST. EACH SPECIES OF WASP HELPS KEEP A WHOLE CHAIN OF ANIMALS ALIVE. IN THE SAME WAY, EACH HUMAN BEING CONTRIBUTES SOMETHING UNIQUE TO THE REST OF THE WORLD.

DECEMBER 11

THOUGHT FOR THE DAY: I WILL ENJOY THE SPECIAL THINGS I BRING TO LIFE.

DECEMBER 12

HERE ARE A FEW TIPS TO KEEP IN MIND TODAY (AND EVERY DAY!) TO HELP YOU TO MAKE AND KEEP FRIENDS:

1. **B**E ACCEPTING OF YOUR DIFFERENCES!

2. **B**E A GOOD LISTENER.

3. **R**EACH OUT. **D**ON'T WAIT FOR SOMEONE ELSE TO MAKE THE FIRST MOVE.

4. **B**E HONEST AND TELL THE TRUTH ABOUT YOUR FEELINGS.

5. **S**HARE YOUR GOOD TIMES AND YOUR HARD TIMES.

THOUGHT FOR THE DAY: **F**RIENDSHIPS MUST BE TENDED TO WITH LOVE AND CARE IF THEY ARE TO GROW AND LAST.

346

UNSCRAMBLE THE FOLLOWING SENTENCE ABOUT LOVE:

EVOL

KEMAS EHT

DROWL OG

NAORUD!

DECEMBER

13

💡

THOUGHT FOR THE DAY:

TODAY **I** WILL REMEMBER THAT LOVE IS THE GREATEST MIRACLE OF ALL.

ANSWER: LOVE MAKES THE WORLD GO AROUND!

DECEMBER 14

HERE'S A FUN JOKE TO
TELL A FRIEND TODAY:

KNOCK KNOCK.
WHO'S THERE?
KUMQUAT.
KUMQUAT WHO?
KUMQUAT MAY, WE'LL
ALWAYS BE FRIENDS!

THOUGHT FOR THE DAY: A TRUE FRIEND WILL
LOVE AND SUPPORT ME
IN THE GOOD TIMES
AND THE HARD TIMES.

HERE ARE SOME FUN SYMBOLS TO DECODE:

THOUGHT FOR THE DAY:

WHEN **I** EXPRESS MYSELF IN MY OWN WAY, **I** CREATE A MEMORABLE DAY!

ANSWER: I LOVE TO BE CREATIVE!

DECEMBER

16

UNSCRAMBLE THE FOLLOWING POSITIVE AFFIRMATION:

BETTER GET I WAY EVERY IN DAY BETTER AND EVERY

THOUGHT FOR THE DAY: **T**ODAY **I** WILL WATCH FOR SIGNS OF IMPROVEMENT IN MYSELF.

ANSWER: EVERY DAY I GET BETTER AND BETTER IN EVERY WAY.

HANUKKAH, THE JEWISH FEAST OF LIGHTS, BEGINS AT SUNDOWN AROUND THIS TIME OF YEAR.

DECEMBER 17

LIGHT A CANDLE IN YOUR HOUSE ON HANUKKAH, EVEN IF YOU AREN'T JEWISH, AND CELEBRATE ALL OF THE GIFTS THAT LIGHT UP YOUR WORLD!

THOUGHT FOR THE DAY: TAKING SOME TIME TO COUNT MY BLESSINGS HELPS ME TO APPRECIATE EVERYTHING MORE.

DECEMBER 18

START A LAUGHING BULLETIN BOARD AND POST IT IN YOUR HOUSE OR BEDROOM WITH CARTOONS, PHOTOGRAPHS, AND PICTURES THAT GIVE YOU AND OTHERS A LIFT!

THOUGHT FOR THE DAY: **B**RINGING GOOD CHEER TO OTHERS IS ONE OF THE FASTEST WAYS TO BRING IT TO MYSELF!

HERE IS A SHORT HAIKU TO KEEP IN MIND. **I**T WILL GIVE YOU THREE WAYS TO STAY HEALTHY INSIDE AND OUT:

DECEMBER
19

EAT THE VERY BEST.
EACH NIGHT GET PLENTY OF REST.
WELCOME SELF AS GUEST.

THOUGHT FOR THE DAY: **S**TAYING HEALTHY IS VERY IMPORTANT TO ME.

DECEMBER 20

No matter how old you are, you need to have some fun and laughter every day. Here are three new ways to say **PLAY**.

INDONESIAN — **B**ERMAIN (BUR-MINE)
POLISH — **G**RAĆ (GROCK)
ITALIAN — **G**IOCARE (JO-CA-**RAY**)

THOUGHT FOR THE DAY: HUMOR AND PLAY BRING HAPPINESS MY WAY!

THERE IS AN ANCIENT EGYPTIAN MYTH ABOUT A BEAUTIFUL BIRD CALLED THE PHOENIX. THE PHOENIX LIVED FOR 500 YEARS AND WAS THEN CONSUMED BY FIRE.

BUT INSTEAD OF DYING, IT ROSE FROM ITS OWN ASHES AND BECAME EVEN STRONGER AND MORE BEAUTIFUL THAN BEFORE!

DECEMBER 21

THOUGHT FOR THE DAY:

WHEN I MAKE A MISTAKE, I WILL THINK OF THE PHOENIX, AND RISE FROM THE ASHES TO BECOME EVEN STRONGER!

THE ANCIENT CHINESE PHILOSOPHER LAO-TZU SAID, "TO SEE WHAT A THING WILL BE WHEN IT IS STILL A SEED — THAT IS GENIUS!"

DECEMBER 22

WHAT SEEDS OF YOUR OWN GENIUS ARE WAITING TO BE PLANTED TODAY?

THOUGHT FOR THE DAY:

TODAY I WILL LOOK FOR WAYS TO LET MORE OF MY INNER GENIUS FLOURISH.

WHAT IS THE MOST UNHAPPY MAMMAL IN THE WORLD?

DECEMBER
23

THOUGHT FOR THE DAY:

TODAY I WILL REMEMBER THAT LIFE IS TOO IMPORTANT TO BE TAKEN SO SERIOUSLY!

ANSWER: A RHINO-SERIOUS.

DECEMBER
24

FILL IN THE BLANKS AND THINK ABOUT THIS IMPORTANT IDEA ABOUT HABITS AND THE FUTURE:

TH - - - H - S F - R -
H - - - TS, A - D
H - B - T - F - R -
O - R F - - U - E.

THOUGHT FOR THE DAY:

A GOOD HABIT TODAY CREATES A BETTER FUTURE TOMORROW.

ANSWER: THOUGHTS FORM HABITS, AND HABITS FORM OUR FUTURE.

TODAY IS CHRISTMAS.

DECEMBER 25

MANY CHRISTIANS EXCHANGE GIFTS ON THIS DAY TO CELEBRATE THE BIRTH OF JESUS. MAKE SOMEONE A GIFT FROM YOUR HEART TODAY—A DRAWING, LETTER, OR SOME OTHER FORM OF SELF-EXPRESSION.

THOUGHT FOR THE DAY: MOST PEOPLE AGREE—THE GREATEST GIFTS ARE THOSE THAT COME FROM THE HEART.

PRACTICE BEING A GIVER TODAY!

DECEMBER 26

PAMPER OTHERS: **D**O A CHORE FOR THEM, MAKE THEM A SMALL TREAT, READ ALOUD TO THEM, OR SURPRISE THEM WITH SOMETHING UNEXPECTED! **T**HEY WILL LOVE IT AND YOU WILL FEEL GREAT TOO!

THOUGHT FOR THE DAY: **O**NE OF THE GREATEST REASONS WE LIVE IS TO GIVE!

DID YOU KNOW THAT WHATEVER YOU THINK ABOUT THE MOST GROWS IN POWER?

DECEMBER

27

POSITIVE THOUGHTS HELP YOUR MIND TO EXPAND, AND FEARFUL OR NEGATIVE THOUGHTS CAUSE YOUR MIND TO CONTRACT.

THOUGHT FOR THE DAY:

TODAY **I** WILL PICTURE MY MIND CONTINUING TO EXPAND LIKE A GALAXY!

361

DECEMBER
28

ASK SOMEONE THIS
"QUIZZICAL QUESTION"
TODAY:

WHICH WOULD
YOU RATHER
BE—A YES, A
NO, OR A
MAYBE—AND
WHY?

THOUGHT
FOR THE DAY:

IT'S FUN TO TRY ON
LOTS OF DIFFERENT
MENTAL PERSPECTIVES!

THIS IS THE **C**HINESE SIGN FOR FRIENDSHIP.

DECEMBER 29

TRY YOUR HAND AT WRITING OUT THE FOUR CHARACTERS THAT SYMBOLIZE THE GIFT OF FRIENDSHIP. **M**AKE COPIES AND HAND THEM OUT TO YOUR FRIENDS TODAY.

THOUGHT FOR THE DAY: **T**HERE IS NO SUCH THING AS TOO MUCH HAPPINESS OR TOO MANY FRIENDS!

DECEMBER 30

HERE IS AN **I**RISH PROVERB: **F**IRELIGHT WILL NOT LET YOU READ STORIES, BUT IT'S WARM AND YOU WON'T SEE THE DUST ON THE FLOOR.

TALK TO SOMEONE TODAY ABOUT WHAT YOU THINK THIS MEANS.

THOUGHT FOR THE DAY: **I**F YOU LOOK FOR IT, THERE IS SOMETHING GOOD TO BE FOUND IN ALMOST EVERYTHING!

TODAY IS NEW YEAR'S EVE! IT HAS BEEN CELEBRATED SINCE 46 **B.C.** IT IS DEDICATED TO THE ROMAN GOD JANUS, THE GOD OF DOORS AND BEGINNINGS. THE SYMBOL OF JANUS IS A HEAD WITH TWO FACES—ONE LOOKING FORWARD AND ONE LOOKING BACKWARD.

DECEMBER
31

MAY YOU LOOK BACK AND SEE THE ACHIEVEMENTS YOU MADE LAST YEAR, AND FORWARD TO THE MANY DREAMS THAT ARE STILL TO COME!

THOUGHT FOR THE DAY:

TODAY I WILL LOOK BACK ON THE ACHIEVEMENTS I MADE LAST YEAR, AND FORWARD TO THE MANY DREAMS THAT ARE STILL TO COME!

365

Decoding Morse Code

Draw the dots and dashes of Morse Code to spell words. Put space between letters to make it clear where each letter begins and ends.

A	• —	J	• — — —	S	• • •
B	— • • •	K	— • —	T	—
C	— • — •	L	• — • •	U	• • —
D	— • •	M	— —	V	• • • —
E	•	N	— •	W	• — —
F	• • — •	O	— — —	X	— • • —
G	— — •	P	• — — •	Y	— • — —
H	• • • •	Q	— — • —	Z	— — • •
I	• •	R	• — •		

DECODING THE NOUGHTS AND CROSSES CODE

THE NOUGHTS AND CROSSES CODE SUBSTITUTES SYMBOLS FOR LETTERS. BASED ON THE TIC-TAC-TOE GRID, DOTS ARE PUT IN PLACE OF THE LETTERS.

A B C	D E F	G H I
J K L	M N	O P Q
R S T	U V W	X Y Z

FOR EXAMPLE, **FRIEND** IS:

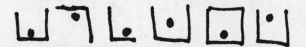

SECRET NUMBER CODE

LOCATE THE FIRST DIGIT OF EACH NUMBER IN THE LEFT-HAND COLUMN. LOCATE THE SECOND DIGIT IN THE TOP ROW. YOU'LL FIND THE LETTER WHERE THEY MEET.

(FOR EXAMPLE: **F** IS 21, **U** IS 51, **N** IS 344)

	1	2	3	4	5
1	A	B	C	D	E
2	F	G	H	I	J
3	K	L	M	N	O
4	P	Q	R	S	T
5	U	V	W	X	Y

TO DECODE MESSAGES IN THE
E-Z SECRET LANGUAGE,
SIMPLY CROSS OUT "**EZ**"
WHEREVER IT APPEARS, THEN
READ THE WORDS MADE BY
THE REMAINING LETTERS.

Compatible Books by Diane Loomans

For Children

The Lovables in the Kingdom of Self-Esteem

Positively Mother Goose
(coauthors, Karen Kolberg and Julia Loomans)

The Lovables
(a board book for young children)

For Parents and Teachers

Full Esteem Ahead
(coauthor, Julia Loomans)

The Laughing Classroom
(coauthor, Karen Kolberg)